Consent, Stealthing and Desire-Based Contracting in the Criminal Law

Consent, Stealthing and Desire-Based Contracting in the Criminal Law examines the inconsistencies in the definitions of consent in sexual encounters by examining emerging sex crimes alongside changing community values and the changing legal definitions of consent in sexual offending, focusing on common law and civil law countries.

This book distinguishes itself through the use of empirically validated research strategies and an in-depth analysis of current legislative regimes. It argues that desire and pleasure are largely ignored by legal consent definitions, despite its importance in sexuality more broadly. Using two case studies of emerging forms of sexual offending, the criminalisation of sadomasochistic sexual practices and the offence of 'stealthing', it examines how the law is both a blunt and underutilised instrument in the policing of people's sexual relationships. The presence or absence of consent can change a lawful sexual act between two people into a serious crime with potentially devastating consequences to both survivor and offender. Yet there remains no consistent definition of consent applied within and between legal jurisdictions across the world. A comparative analysis reveals parallels between common law countries and civil law countries. The book also provides a brief history of the use of the term 'consent' in relation to sexual offending and examines definitional and sociological requirements of conceptual consent across history.

Covering jurisdictions in the US, UK, and Australia, providing an innovative resource on issues relating to consent presented in an accessible way, this book will appeal to students and researchers of criminal justice, criminal law, criminology, sociology, and gender studies.

Brianna Chesser is a senior lecturer in Criminology and Justice at RMIT University. She is admitted as a barrister and solicitor of the Supreme Court of Victoria and a solicitor of the High Court of Australia. She is also a practicing chartered clinical psychologist, a forensic psychology registrar, and a senior fellow of the Higher Education Academy. Chesser is the principal solicitor of Chesser Lawyers and practices predominantly in criminal law, and she is the principal clinical psychologist of Invoke Psychology.

Nadia David is an associate lecturer in Criminal Justice and Criminology at RMIT University and is currently undertaking a PhD at Monash University looking at concepts of consent in the criminal law. A lawyer and former police officer and Commonwealth public servant, Nadia is now the co-convenor for the Victorian EMILY's List Action Group and is working on her first crime novel from her home in north-east Victoria.

April Zahra is admitted as a solicitor of the Supreme Court of Victoria and is a lawyer at Slater and Gordon Lawyers. April completed a Bachelor of Laws and a Bachelor of Global Studies (Honours) at Australian Catholic University. April completed her Honour's dissertation on elements of consent and the criminal law and has published in this area.

Routledge Frontiers of Criminal Justice

Professionalism in Probation
Making sense of marketisation
Matt Tidmarsh

Policing Child Sexual Abuse
Failure, corruption and reform in Queensland
Paul Bleakley

Collaboration and Innovation in Criminal Justice
An activity theory alternative to offender rehabilitation
Paulo Rocha

Genetic Surveillance and Crime Control
Social, cultural and political perspectives
Helen Machado and Rafaela Granja

Impending Challenges to Penal Moderation in Germany and France
A strained restraint
Edited by Kirstin Drenkhahn, Fabien Jobard and Tobias Singelnstein

Policing and Boundaries in a Violent Society
A South African case study
Guy Lamb

Consent, Stealthing and Desire-Based Contracting in the Criminal Law
Brianna Chesser, Nadia David and April Zahra

For more information about this series, please visit: www.routledge.com/Routledge-Frontiers-of-Criminal-Justice/book-series/RFCJ

Consent, Stealthing and Desire-Based Contracting in the Criminal Law

Brianna Chesser, Nadia David and April Zahra

Routledge
Taylor & Francis Group
LONDON AND NEW YORK

First published 2022
by Routledge
2 Park Square, Milton Park, Abingdon, Oxon OX14 4RN

and by Routledge
605 Third Avenue, New York, NY 10158

Routledge is an imprint of the Taylor & Francis Group, an informa business

British Library Cataloguing-in-Publication Data
A catalogue record for this book is available from the British Library

Library of Congress Cataloging-in-Publication Data
Names: Chesser, Brianna Jade, author. |
David, Nadia, author. | Zahra, April, author.
Title: Consent, stealthing and desire-based contracting in the
criminal law / Brianna Chesser, Nadia David and April Zahra.
Description: Abingdon, Oxon ; New York, NY : Routledge, 2022. |
Series: Routledge series of frontier justice |
Includes bibliographicalreferences and index.
Identifiers: LCCN 2021041523 (print) | LCCN 2021041524 (ebook) |
ISBN 9780367710705 (hardback) | ISBN 9780367761233 (paperback) |
ISBN 9781003165606 (ebook)
Subjects: LCSH: Sexual consent. |
Rape–Law and legislation. | Sexcrimes–Law and legislation.
Classification: LCC K5194 .C44 2022 (print) |
LCC K5194 (ebook) | DDC345/.0253–dc23/eng/20211006
LC record available at https://lccn.loc.gov/2021041523
LC ebook record available at https://lccn.loc.gov/2021041524

ISBN: 978-0-367-71070-5 (hbk)
ISBN: 978-0-367-76123-3 (pbk)
ISBN: 978-1-003-16560-6 (ebk)

DOI: 10.4324/9781003165606

Typeset in Times New Roman
by Newgen Publishing UK

Contents

1 Historical context of consent

Historical context

The laws surrounding the concept of consent have been evolving since their first known iteration. As perceptions regarding acceptable sexual conduct have evolved, society has responded by ensuring the law codifies and reflects these changing standards.[1]

The historical context of consent continues to influence its contemporary formation and impacts the enforcement of consent laws in Western common law countries. For the purposes of this volume, we refer to consent as the legal agreement, freely given by an adult with legal capacity to enter into sexual relations with another person.

The historical conceptualisation of women as property – first of their fathers and then of their husbands – has contributed to long-standing difficulties with recognising forms of non-consensual sexual activity and has perpetuated rape myths that still influence perceptions in contemporary times.

This chapter will consider the historical context and development of consent law.

Rape as a property offence

Historically, the crime of rape was regarded not as a crime against a person but as a crime against property.[2] This understanding of rape

1 James Roffee, 'When Yes Actually Means Yes: Confusing Messages and Criminalising Consent' in Anastasia Powell, Nicola Henry and Asher Flynn (eds), *Rape Justice* (Palgrave Macmillan) 72, 74.

2 Carol E. Tracy et al, 'Rape and Sexual Assault in the Legal System' (Conference Paper, National Research Council of the National Academies Panel on Measuring Rape and Sexual Assault in the Bureau of Justice Statistics Household Surveys Committee on

DOI: 10.4324/9781003165606-1

was reinforced by the development of the marital rape immunity and the common law characterisation of rape as 'carnal knowledge'.[3] It was not until a wave of legal reform in the late twentieth century that the modern-day construction of consent as free agreement between any two persons, was developed.

In medieval times, 'rape' was regarded as 'ravishment or abduction of unmarried women without paternal consent'.[4] In this context, a woman's reproductive capacity was regarded as property and was fundamental to establishing 'patriarchal inheritance rights'.[5] Generally, property ownership of a woman's sexuality belonged to her father, which then transferred to her husband, usually pursuant to an arranged marriage.[6] The woman's untouched sexuality was the key asset in this transaction, and rape of an unmarried virgin was considered theft of this chattel. Accordingly, the offence was purely designed to protect the economic interest of men facilitating these transactions.[7]

Under this understanding of rape, unmarried women could only be considered to have been raped if they were virgins and rape could not be perpetrated by a married woman's spouse, who was considered to possess ownership of her sexuality.[8] Moreover, men could not be raped, rape could not occur between the same sex, rape of orifices other than the vagina were not recognised, and rape was not a crime if the woman was not a virgin.[9] These conditions reflected the notion that rape was a crime against a woman's chasity, and as non-traditional forms of rape did not impact this virtue, they were not recognised as an offence.[10] Therefore, rape was not considered a crime against a person but was more akin to the offence of trespassing.[11]

The historical classification of rape as a property offence was also heavily influenced by religion. The Babylonian Code of Hammurabi (c1755–1750), which is long considered to be the first written law,

National Statistics, 5 June 2012). www.womenslawproject.org/wp-content/uploads/2016/04/Rape-and-Sexual-Assault-in-the-Legal-System-FINAL.pdf.

3 Anastasia Powell et al, 'Meanings of "Sex" and "Consent": The Persistence of Rape Myths in Victorian Rape Law' (2013) 22(2) *Griffith Law Review* 456, 460.

4 Simon Bronitt and Bernadette McSherry, *Principles of Criminal Law* (Thomson Reuters (Professional) Australia, 4th ed, 2017) 656.

5 Tracy et al (n 2) 4.

6 Ibid.

7 Ibid.

8 Ibid.

9 Ibid.

10 Ibid 5.

11 Arthur S. Chancellor, *Investigating Sexual Assault Cases* (Jones & Bartlett Publishers, 2012) 7.

described the crime of rape as 'the theft of virginity, an embezzlement of his daughter's fair price on the market'.[12] These ancient laws defined rape as 'an offense in which the theft of a woman's virginity represented a crime against her father, in that his daughter's marketability had been devalued'.[13]

Pursuant to this code, if a virgin was raped, she was not culpable. On the other hand, a married woman was someone considered to have precipitated the attack.[14] Specially, ancient Hebrew law dictated that if a man raped a woman within the walls of a city, and that woman was betrothed to another man, both the woman and the rapist would be subjected to the same punishment – death by stoning.[15] The woman was equally culpable in this situation as it was considered that if she had screamed, then she would have attracted attention and been helped.[16] The rapists' fate ultimately stemmed from the fact that he had 'humbled his neighbour'.[17] On the other hand, if the same woman was assaulted outside of the city walls or whilst labouring in the fields, only the rapist was put to death. This was because, in this situation, it was reasonable that nobody could hear the woman scream for help.[18]

If an unattached virgin was raped, the outcome was entirely different – in this situation neither the woman nor the rapist was put to death.[19] Instead, the rapist was required to pay an amount of compensation to the woman's husband or father, with the exact amount being dependent on the woman's economic position or standing in society, and therefore the desirability of an 'exclusive sexual relationship'.[20] The sum was paid directly to the dominant male in the female's life (usually the husband or father) as they were considered to be 'wronged' by the assault.[21]

Rape was therefore considered the theft of sexual property under the ownership of someone other than the rapist, where women were deemed to be private property whose value was determined by their economic

12 Ibid.

13 Lane Kirkland Gillespie and Laura King, 'Legislative Origins, Reforms and Future Directions' in Tara N. Richards and Catherine D. Marcum (eds), *Sexual Victimization: Then and Now* (SAGE, 2014) 15, 16.

14 Chancellor (n 11) 8.

15 Bruce A. MacFarlane, *Historical Development of the Offence of Rape* (Wood and Peck, 1993).

16 Ibid.

17 Ibid.

18 Ibid.

19 Ibid.

20 Ibid.

21 Ibid.

standing and sexual and reproductive capacities. From a legal viewpoint, in having sexual intercourse with a woman who was not the property of a man, that man was guilty of trespassing on the property of whoever did 'own' the woman as property. The man therefore stole or trespassed on property to which he possessed no legal right. Ultimately, rape law was intended 'to regulate competing male interests in controlling sexual access to females',[22] rather than protecting women's autonomy and control over their own bodies and sexuality.

The notion of the offence of rape as representing a property offence has been further promoted by conflicts that have occurred throughout the ages. For instance, women were considered 'spoils' of war, along with cattle and other chattels.[23] It was only as early as the fourteenth century that rape was no longer officially encouraged in these arenas; however, it was tolerated and accepted by wartime officials, as it was considered that rape prior to battle would operate to boost solider morale and that rape after the battle was won, functioned as a reward.[24] The raping of women was further contemplated as a way for a victorious army to humiliate the 'property' of a defeated nation,[25] and as a means for governments and generals to 'pay' soldiers for their service.[26]

Development of rape law from the tenth century onwards

Prior to the Norman Conquest of 1066, under ancient Saxon laws, the penalty for rape was cited as death and dismemberment.[27] Under tenth-century English law, a man guilty of raping a woman who was a virgin was sentenced to death and all of his land and capital were passed on to the victim's family.[28] However, the punishment of death and dismemberment was only applicable to 'the man who raped a highborn, propertied virgin who lived under the protection of a powerful lord', again

22 Matthew R. Lyon, 'No Means No?: Withdrawal of Consent during Intercourse and the Continuing Evolution of the Definition of Rape' (2004) 95(1) *The Journal of Criminal Law & Criminology* 277, 282.

23 Kelly D. Askin, 'Prosecuting Wartime Rape and Other Gender-Related Crimes under International Law: Extraordinary Advances, Enduring Obstacles' (2003) 21(2) *Berkeley Journal of International Law* 288, 296; Hannah Tonkin, 'Rape in the International Arena: The Evolution of Autonomy and Consent' (2004) 23(2) *University of Tasmania Law Review* 243.

24 Askin (n 23) 288, 296; Tonkin (n 23) 243.

25 Chancellor (n 11) 7.

26 Ibid.

27 Ibid 9.

28 Gillespie and King (n 13) 15, 16.

reflecting the socioeconomic class divide at the time.[29] The method of trial commonly cited during this time was one of trial by combat, and it was not until the twelfth century that a raped virgin could file an action for 'appeal' which would instead occur via a trial before a jury in the King's Court.[30] For such an appeal to have a chance of success, the woman would have to, immediately after the offence, display her injuries to a man of good repute.[31] It was expected that there would be evidence of blood and torn garments, providing early confirmation of rape myths that are still influential today.[32]

It is difficult to pinpoint the exact point in time where rape was first properly recognised and reflected by law and society. Partly, this is attributed to the fact that English rape law did not adequately define 'rape' and the necessary elements of proof, and also because the crime of rape was often conflated with the crime of ravishment, a 'trespass' or private wrong against an individual.[33] Between the twelfth and sixteenth centuries, three statutes are typically cited as pertaining to rape, being the First and Second Statutes of Westminster (1275 and 1285) and an Elizabethan Statute (1576).[34] However, some consider that the 1275 statute should not be included in this list because it is properly considered a law against ravishment and that the other statutes, while establishing a prohibition primarily against woman or child rape, did not define the term or explain what is required to prove such an offence.[35] There is also uncertainty about the exact scope of the offence in light of inconsistencies with the Latin translation.[36]

The State of Westminster 1275 provided that 'The King prohibiteth that none do ravish [...] any Maiden within Age'.[37] This statute displaced any consideration of the woman's virginity and constructed the crime as sexual intercourse with a female against her will and a female under the age of 12.[38] Moreover, a woman no longer had to commence proceedings immediately following the assault.[39] Subsequently, the offence of rape

29 Ibid.
30 MacFarlane (n 15).
31 Ibid.
32 Ibid.
33 Anne Leah Greenfield, *Interpreting Sexual Violence, 1660–1800* (Taylor & Francis Group, 1st ed, 2015) 24.
34 Ibid.
35 Ibid.
36 MacFarlane (n 15).
37 Carolyn Cocca, *Jailbait: The Politics of Statutory Rape Laws in the United States* (State University of New York Press, 1st ed, 2004) 10.
38 MacFarlane (n 15).
39 Ibid.

was made a capital one under the 1285 statute and the age of the female was lowered to ten in the 1576 statute: 'if any person shall unlawfully and carnally know and abuse any woman-child under the age of ten years old, every such unlawful and carnal knowledge shall be a felony'.[40] The 1576 statute was enacted with the aim of 'repressing of the most wicked and felonious Rapes of Ravishments of Woman, Maids, Wives and Damsels'.[41] However, in effect, this essentially reproduced the thirteenth-century laws already in existence and did not further define or explain the circumstances necessary to prove the offence. The 1576 statute acted as England's rape law until the nineteenth century.[42]

The language utilised in these English laws was essentially the same language adopted by the statutes effected in colonial America, with variation among states as to the age of consent.[43] Similarly to the English model, the motivation behind these laws at the time was not about the ability of a woman to consent but was about protecting white females and their premarital chastity, which was a valuable commodity.[44] For example, Justice William J. Brennan noted in *Michael M. v Superior Court of Sonoma County* that 'because their chastity was considered particularly precious, those young women were felt to be uniquely in need of the state's protection'.[45] However, these American statutes only applied to white females, as black females were usually formally enslaved and their sexuality was not deemed in need of legal protection.[46] Accordingly, black females were only commodified in terms of their services and childbearing capacity, and not in respect of their chastity or virtue.[47]

Criminal law statutes in most jurisdictions did not advance until the twelfth and thirteenth centuries. The first significant advancement in England enabled a rape victim to file a civil suit against the perpetrator, followed by a trial by jury.[48] During the thirteenth century, the definition of rape also evolved to include the rape of 'matrons, nuns and widows, concubines, and prostitutes, as well as the statutory rape of children'.[49] These advancements signified the first significant progression towards

40 Cocca (n 37) 10.
41 Greenfield (n 33) 25.
42 Ibid.
43 Cocca (n 37) 10, 11.
44 Ibid.
45 Ibid; *Michael M. v Superior Court of Sonoma County* 450 US 464 [1981] at 494–495.
46 Cocca (n 37) 10, 11.
47 Ibid.
48 Gillespie and King (n 13) 15, 16.
49 Ibid.

rape being viewed as a public safety issue rather than a property offence.[50]

While the concept of consent was arguably anticipated in the thirteenth century, its role in governing lawful sexual intercourse was not clear until the 1845 case of *R v Camplin*.[51] In this case, the complainant was penetrated by the accused whist in an intoxicated state. The House of Lords held that rape could occur if the penetration took place without a victim's consent and against the victim's will. This case established that sexual intercourse that is 'against her will' is non-consensual, rather than a strict requirement of force or injury.

The offence of rape has since continued to develop through the interaction between the courts and Parliament. Modern constructions of the meaning of consent will be discussed in Chapter 2.

Age of consent

Historically, similar to the issue of sexual violence, the age that two individuals could engage in 'sexual union' was an issue for an individual's family to decide, or was treated as a matter of 'tribal custom'.[52] Traditionally, the issue of capacity usually coincided with the onset of puberty, symbolised by menstruation in girls and the appearance of pubic hair in boys (usually between the ages of 12 to 14).[53] It was also generally accepted that sexual union could only occur following a marital union or ceremonial equivalent.

In Republican Rome, the age of consent and marriage (two related concepts) were considered private matters to be dealt with by the families involved in the union.[54] It was not until the first century that the state began to regulate these matters and marriage then became a two-step process: (1) a betrothal which consisted of a legally enforceable agreement between the heads of the households and (2) the marriage itself.[55] However, if a woman was not yet 'of age', she could only be betrothed with the consent of her father.

In medieval Europe, the traditional age of puberty – and therefore capacity for marriage – was between 12 and 14. However, according

50 Ibid.
51 *R v Camplin* (1845) 1 Cox 22, confirmed in *R v Fletcher* (1859) 8 Cox 131.
52 Vern L. Bullough, 'Age of Consent' (2018) *Encyclopedia of Children and Childhood in History and Society* (Article, 27 June 2018) www.encyclopedia.com/social-sciences-and-law/law/law/age-consent.
53 Ibid.
54 Ibid.
55 Ibid.

to Gratian,[56] consent was only 'meaningful' if a child was older than seven.[57] These marriages would generally be recognised as legitimate if neither party sought an annulment before reaching puberty, or if they had already 'consummated' the marriage.[58] It was therefore possible for a husband to rape his wife prior to the time she reached puberty and the marriage would be recognised as legitimate due to the act of consummation – consensual or not.[59]

These historical concepts governing the age and circumstances of consent were carried over into English common law. The American colonies also followed the English ideals; however, the law was less stringently followed in this regard.[60] In 1885 England, feminists and reformers together successfully lobbied Parliament to raise the age of consent to 16. This also prompted American reformers to act and by the 1920s, the age of consent was raised in every state in the United States, ranging from 14 to 18.[61]

Rape as carnal knowledge

By the eighteenth century, the English courts, influenced by other statutory sex crimes, recognised the common law offence of rape.[62] The crime of rape was defined narrowly as 'carnal knowledge', being the penetration of the vagina by a penis which was deemed complete only upon proof of penetration.[63]

This iteration of rape was limited to non-consensual penetration of the vagina, however slight, by the penis, consequently excluding various forms of unwanted sexual conduct. Neither complete penetration nor ejaculation was necessary.[64]

There were five elements required to prosecute the offence of common law rape: the act had to be criminal, involve carnal knowledge, victimise a woman, be committed using force and the force had to be against the victim's will.[65] It was therefore limited to intercourse between a man and a woman who were not married and centred around the degree of force

56 Gratian was the influential founder of canon law in the twelfth century.
57 Bullough (n 52).
58 Ibid.
59 Ibid.
60 Ibid.
61 Ibid.
62 Bronitt and McSherry (n 4) 656.
63 Ibid 657.
64 *Holland v R* (1993) 67 ALJR 946.
65 Gillespie and King (n 13) 15, 17.

utilised and the ensuing resistance shown by the victim.[66] A successful prosecution required evidence of physical harm and corroboration of the victim's claim.[67]

Accordingly, this definition of rape did not include sexual penetration of other bodily orifices, such as the anus.[68] These other acts of non-consensual penetrative conduct were dealt with as other offences, for example, non-consensual penile penetration of the anus was known as 'buggery'.[69] Similarly, the forcible insertion of physical objects into the vagina or anus, or forcible oral intercourse was classed as indecent assault (or in more serious cases, assault occasioning actual bodily harm or aggravated assault).[70] A case of indecent assault not involving serious bodily harm carried a maximum penalty of five years' imprisonment.[71]

Generally, the offence of rape was limited to instances of conscious refusal or where a woman was unconscious or unable to consent,[72] for example, where a woman was beaten into submission or where the perpetrator spiked the victim's drink. Moreover, the common law definition of rape also failed to recognise rape between members of the same sex. That is, the notion that rape could only be committed by a male perpetrator against a woman obviously omitted instances of rape between members of the same sex.[73]

Common law rape was therefore only deemed to be committed where the act of penetration was against a woman's will. This understanding of rape was evidently flawed, as it failed to recognise all forms of unwanted penetration and also omitted instances where victims would commonly freeze and exert no verbal or physical objection to the unwanted sexual activity.[74] Common law rape also encompassed various irrefutable presumptions, including that a husband could not rape his wife.[75] However, a woman could be convicted as an accomplice to an act of rape performed by a man,[76] and a boy under the age of 14 years was incapable of rape.[77]

66 Ibid.
67 Ibid.
68 Brianna Chesser and April Zahra, 'Stealthing: A Criminal Offence?' (2019) 31(2) *Current Issues in Criminal Justice* 217, 221.
69 See *Crimes Act 1958* (Vic) s 68 (now repealed), *Crimes Act 1900* (NSW) s 79.
70 Thalia Anthony et al, *Waller and Williams Criminal Law Texts and Cases* (LexisNexis Butterworths, 12th ed, 2013) 108.
71 Ibid.
72 Ibid 107.
73 Ibid.
74 Chesser and Zahra (n 68) 217, 221.
75 Anthony et al (n 70) 108.
76 *R v Ram and Ram* (1893) 17 Cox CC 609.
77 *R v Waite* [1892] 2 QB 600.

The United Kingdom common law definition of rape formed the basis for the common law definition in a number of jurisdictions internationally, including the United States and Australia.

Mistake and fraud

Under the common law definition of rape, there are only very limited circumstances that mistake, or fraud could vitiate consent to sexual activity.[78] This position was made clear early on by Stephen J in the *R v Clarence* (1888) 22 QBD 23:

> The only sorts of fraud which so far destroy the effect of a woman's consent as to convert a connection consented to in fact into a rape are frauds as to the nature of the act itself, or as to the identity of the person who does the act.[79]

This position was subsequently accepted by the High Court of Australia in *Papadimitropoulos v The Queen.*[80] In this case, the accused procured a young woman who did not speak English to repeatedly have sexual intercourse with him by deceiving the woman into believing they were legally married. The accused took the woman to a marriage registry under the ruse that they were to be married. The woman brought three family members who also did not speak English to witness the marriage – however in actuality the ceremony merely involved the signing of a marriage licence. Following the fake ceremony, the accused told the woman that they were married, gave her a wedding ring and consistently represented to third parties that they were married. The woman had not intended to have sexual intercourse until she was married.

The High Court unanimously decided that the accused's conduct did not constitute rape under Australian law – keeping in line with the 'judicial resistance' to the idea that consent to sexual intercourse can be vitiated by fraud or mistake.[81] The High Court held that where a person agrees to sex under the mistaken belief that they are married to the

78 Andrew Dyer, 'Mistakes That Negate Apparent Consent' (2019) 43 *Criminal Law Journal* 159.

79 *R v Clarence* (1888) 22 QBD 23, 43.

80 *Papadimitropoulos v The Queen* (1957) 98 CLR 249.

81 *Papadimitropoulos v The Queen* (1957) 98 CLR 249, 255; Chesser and Zahra (n 68) 217, 224; Jonathan Crowe 'Fraud and Consent in Australian Rape Law' (2014) 38(4) *Criminal Law Journal* 236, 237.

accused, the act does not involve a mistake as to the 'nature and character of the act' so as to have a vitiating effect.[82]

The Court confirmed the earlier decision of *R v Clarence* that only certain forms of mistake or fraud could amount to rape, being where there was mistake about the identity of the person or about the fundamental nature of the act.[83] In respect of this second category, the High Court expressed that this category is to be interpreted narrowly, involving only instances where the fraud or mistake specifically relates to the purpose of the sexual act. The High Court also confirmed that in cases of fraud in rape law, the focus should be properly placed on the victim's state of mind rather than the deceptive conduct of the accused.

Prior to these decisions, the courts were hesitant to accept that a complainant's consent was not real in these circumstances. For example, a number of nineteenth-century English cases supported that it was not rape where a man impersonated a woman's husband and subsequently had intercourse with her.[84]

Marital rape immunity

A seventeenth-century by-product of the property-based offence of consent was the development of the martial rape immunity, which granted a husband 'immunity' from prosecution of rape committed against his wife.

The origin of the marital rape immunity is widely traced to the views of eighteenth-century English judge and jurist Sir Matthew Hale, published in *The History of the Pleas of the Crown* (1736):

> The husband cannot be guilty of a rape committed by himself upon his lawful wife, for by their mutual matrimonial consent and contract the wife hath given up herself in this kind unto her husband, which she cannot retract.[85]

Hale therefore promoted the view that sexual relations within marriage were governed by 'implied' terms of the marriage contract.[86] Therefore

82 *Papadimitropoulos v The Queen* (1957) 98 CLR 249.
83 *R v Clarence* (1888) 22 QBD 23.
84 *R v Jackson* (1822) Russ and Ry 487; *R v Saunders* (1838) 9 Car & P 265; *R v Williams* (1838) 8 Car & P 286; *R v Barrow* (1868) LR 1 CCR 156.
85 Matthew Hale, *The History of the Pleas of the Crown* (Payne, 1800) 629.
86 Bronitt and McSherry (n 4) 659.

by entering into the marriage, a wife gave implied consent to all further acts of intercourse with her husband.

While Hale cited no authority for his proposition, it is considered that his proposition was likely supported by ecclesiastical law.[87] The logic behind this immunity from an ecclesiastical point of view was that rape of married women by their spouses was not a crime because the law presumed a broad notion of consent to all of a wife's sexual activity through wedding vows. That is, a husband had a 'conjugal right' to sexual intercourse from his wife.[88]

Other theories conclude that the immunity was created because of the common law position which viewed a wife as a husband's property or the marital couple as one 'person' or 'unit'.[89] As espoused by William Blackstone: 'By marriage, the very being or legal existence of woman is suspended, or at least it is incorporated and consolidated into that of a husband'.[90] Moreover, from a policy perspective, the martial rape immunity was viewed as a means of preventing an aggrieved wife from making an allegation of rape against her husband, which would be difficult for him to disprove.

In practice, there were limited exceptions to the operation of the immunity, including that in some circumstances a man could be convicted of raping his wife if he helped another man force sex upon her, and that a husband could also be convicted of 'sodomy' if he inflicted what was considered 'unnatural sex' on his wife.[91] These exceptions were reflective of the notion that rape was only considered harmful when it spoiled a woman's 'virtue' or 'chastity'.[92]

While the marital rape immunity was accepted as a valid legal principle for over 200 years, by the mid-twentieth century (1960s) the immunity became increasingly scrutinised by feminists and academic commentary, which had a direct impact on judicial decision-making.[93]

87 Ibid.

88 Ibid; Michelle J. Anderson, 'Diminishing the Legal Impact of Negative Social Attitudes toward Acquaintance Rape Victims' (2010) 13(4) *New Criminal Law Review: An International and Interdisciplinary Journal* 644, 658.

89 Jed Rubenfeld, 'The Riddle of Rape-by-Deception and the Myth of Sexual Autonomy' (2013) 122(6) *Yale Law Journal* 1372, 1390. See also *Commonwealth v. Chretien*, 417 N.E.2d 1203, 1207 (Mass. 1981) 'It is generally thought [...] that the basis of the spousal exclusion probably lies in the ancient concept of the wife as chattel'.

90 William Blackstone, *Commentaries on the Laws of England* (1765) vol 1, 442–445.

91 Rubenfeld (n 89) 1372, 1391.

92 Ibid.

93 Kos Lesses, '*PGA v. the Queen*: Marital Rape in Australia: The Role of Repetition, Reputation and Fiction in the Common Law' (2014) 37(3) *Melbourne University Law Review* 786, 812.

Judges began to place limitations on the operation of the immunity. For example, judges began to deny the application of the immunity in cases where a husband and wife were separated pursuant to a court order.[94]

By the late 1980s the marital rape immunity was abolished by statute in each Australian jurisdiction.[95] The English common law quickly followed suit in the 1992 decision of *R v R* where the House of Lords promoted the abolishment of the marital rape immunity.[96] In this case, it was not in contention that the accused had violently had sex with his wife, who was living separately to him at the time; rather, the consideration for the court was whether or not a husband was immune in circumstances where the separation was not pursuant to a court order. The trial judge refused to recognise that any immunity existed in modern law. On appeal, the House of Lords affirmed the trial judge's decision, holding that the immunity was a 'common law fiction which has become anachronistic and offensive'.[97]

Around the same time, the High Court in Australia was also considering the place of the marital rape immunity in the Australian common law in the case of *R v L*.[98] This case concerned an accused who was charged and convicted of two counts of rape against his wife. The accused had been charged in South Australia where the marital rape immunity had been abolished by statute. On appeal to the High Court, the accused argued that the South Australian legislation was inconsistent with the operation of the *Family Law Act 1975* (Cth), which allowed the Family Court to make an order relieving a party to a marriage from rendering conjugal rights. The accused submitted that the two provisions were directly inconsistent, as the South Australian Act eliminated the obligation to perform conjugal rights for every married person, and the Commonwealth Act assumed the existence of the obligation (however, the Family Court was able to relieve a party of this obligation by way of its discretionary power). If this argument was accepted, section 109 of the Australian Constitution would render that any inconsistency be resolved in favour of the Commonwealth law.

The High Court ultimately rejected that there was any inconsistency between the provisions and also clarified the status of the immunity (in *obiter*). The majority doubted whether the marital rape immunity had ever been part of the common law, and ultimately observed that

94 Bronitt and McSherry (n 4) 659.
95 Ibid 660.
96 *R v R [1992]* 1 AC 599.
97 Ibid 611.
98 *R v L* (1991) 174 CLR 379.

regardless of its previous inclusion, the marital rape immunity was no longer part of the common law as the Court 'would be justified in refusing to accept a notion that is so out of keeping with the view society now takes of the relationship between the parties to a marriage'.[99]

While the Court in *R v L* expressed their doubt that the immunity had ever been part of the common law,[100] it was unnecessary for them to decide at what point the immunity ceased to be good law. It was not until two decades later that this issue was addressed by the High Court in the case of *PGA v The Queen*.[101]

In 2010, the Director of Public Prosecutions of South Australia charged PGA with a number of sexual offences pertaining to conduct that occurred in 1963, prior to the abolition of the marital rape immunity in South Australia. The High Court upheld the conviction in keeping with the decision in *R v L*, stating that even if the marital rape immunity had existed at some point in time, it had ceased to exist by the time of the enactment of rape as an offence in the *Crimes Consolidation Act 1935* (SA). The majority held that in the common law there was no immunity as in 1963 and consequently, PGA could be found guilty of rape.[102]

In reaching their decision, the majority discussed that Hale's position was not framed in 'absolute terms'.[103] The Court considered that it was well settled that marriage was constituted by the consent of the parties expressed under such circumstances as the law required, but did not require consummation to complete the marriage.[104] The Court also noted that the ecclesiastical courts did not enforce any duty of sexual intercourse between married couples.[105] Therefore, as sexual intercourse was not a prerequisite within marital relations, neither party could be compelled by law to engage in sexual intercourse. Ultimately, the majority concluded that Hale's proposition was unclear, and noted Hale did not cite any prior cases which might be said to support his proposition.[106]

The majority considered that the statutory reform of married womens' rights at this time vastly impacted the common law and concluded:

99 Ibid 390; Bronitt and McSherry (n 4) 661.
100 *R v L* (1991) 174 CLR 379.
101 *PGA v The Queen (2012)* 245 CLR 355.
102 Ibid.
103 Ibid 377, [43].
104 Ibid.
105 Ibid.
106 Ibid.

> By the time of the enactment in 1935 of the [*Criminal Law Consolidation Act* 1935 (SA)], if not earlier (a matter which it is unnecessary to decide here), in Australia local statute law had removed any basis for continued acceptance of Hale's proposition as part of the English common law received in the Australian colonies. Thus, at all times relevant to this appeal, and contrary to Hale's proposition, at common law a husband could be guilty of rape committed by him upon his lawful wife. Lawful marriage to a complainant provided neither a defence to, nor an immunity from, a prosecution for rape.[107]

While the majority doubted that the immunity had ever been part of Australian law, the two dissenting judgements (Heydon and Bell JJ) observed that the immunity had been widely accepted as part of Australian law.[108] This was despite the absence of binding precedent applying the immunity in either Australia or England. In fact, there are only three reported cases that address marital immunity: *R v Clarence* in 1888, *R v Clarke* in 1949, and *R v Miller* in 1954.[109] However, none of these cases actually established the marital immunity as a binding principle of the common law.[110] Nevertheless, Bell J expressed that the lack of binding authority 'does not mean that a rule stated in authoritative texts and accepted and acted upon by the legal profession over many years may not acquire status as law'.[111]

The decision was also influential as it ultimately involved the consideration of the issue of retrospectivity in context of criminal prosecutions.[112] The Court had to consider whether the martial rape immunity ever existed and if so, whether it should be upheld. Ultimately, the majority refused to allow the accused to argue the martial rape immunity as a defence; however, the Court claimed that retrospectivity did not arise and therefore did not take the opportunity to reconcile principles of retrospectivity. Academics consider that the Court missed an opportunity to expand on the understanding of retrospectivity in Australian common law, taking an 'unnecessarily' narrow view of the principle.[113]

107 Ibid 384, [64].

108 Ibid.

109 *R v Clarence* (1888) 22 QBD 23, *R v Clarke* [1949] 2 All ER 448, *R v Miller* [1954] 2 QB 282; Lesses (n 93) 786, 799.

110 Lesses (n 93) 786, 799.

111 *PGA v The Queen* (2012) 245 CLR 355, 437, [222].

112 Kellie Toole, 'Marital Rape: Retrospectivity and the Common Law' (2015) *Criminal Law Journal* 39(6), 286–302.

113 Ibid.

Statutory appeal of the immunity first occurred in South Australia in 1976, followed by Western Australia (1976), Victoria and New South Wales (1981), the Australian Capital Territory (1985), Tasmania (1987), Queensland (1989) and the Northern Territory (1994). All states and territories now expressly abolish the immunity.

Unsurprisingly, the United States similarly recognised a marital rape immunity in early versions of its rape laws. Until the late 1970s, the definition of rape in most American jurisdictions exempted husbands from being prosecuted for raping their wives.[114] The *Model Penal Code* (MPC) revised the common law definition of rape whilst maintaining an absolute marital exemption.[115] This is justified in the commentary to the MPC which states that the marital rape exemption avoids an 'unwanted intrusion of the penal law into the life of the family'.[116] This commentary has been cited as a defence to Hale's eighteenth-century position.[117]

The marital rape immunity was one of the first subjects of feminist critique in America.[118] Following statutory and common law reform in the 1980s, the number of states in which husbands could be prosecuted for raping their wives increased from nine to forty-two.[119] In the present day, marital rape is illegal in all American states; however, the archaic effects of the immunity are still said to impact prosecution in some states.[120]

Towards the concept of consent – human rights

It was not until the mid-nineteenth century that the notion of 'consent' developed as the distinguishing factor between lawful and unlawful sexual activity.[121] In most jurisdictions, the law now recognises that rape and other sexual offences are grounded on a lack of consent, with points of divergence still existing surrounding the specifications of what entails consent, for example, the need for positive resistance or the level of the perpetrator's knowledge of the victim's lack of consent.[122]

114 Lyon (n 22) 277, 282.
115 Ibid.
116 Toole (n 112) 286–302.
117 *Model Penal Code* § 213.1(1) (1980); Lyon (n 22) 277, 282.
118 Lyon (n 22) 277, 283.
119 Ibid.
120 Ibid 284.
121 Bronitt and McSherry (n 4) 656.
122 Vanessa E. Munro, 'From Consent to Coercion' in Clare McGlynn and Vanessa E. Munro (eds), *Rethinking Rape Law: International and Comparative Perspectives* (Taylor & Francis Group) 17, 20.

The development of consent has been largely framed by both principles of liberalism and feminism – in particular, theoretical discussions about how the nature and scope of sexual offences fit in with recognised human rights.[123] In fact, it is considered that all references to 'consent' in international law must be interpreted in a manner consistent with human rights law standard.[124]

Human rights are expressed in international treaties as well as in domestic human rights legislation. Justice P. Kirby in the influential case of *Kitchener* observed that rights to human dignity and privacy are both relevant to how key concepts of criminal responsibility should be understood:

> Every individual has a right to the human dignity of his or her own person. Having sexual intercourse with another, without the consent of that other, amounts to an affront to that other's human dignity and an invasion of the privacy of that person's body and personality.[125]

The notion of human dignity, as cited by Justice Kirby, forms the basis of international human rights and is the key consideration in international criminal law.[126] For example, influential international law treaties such as the Universal Declaration of Human Rights (UDHR), the International Covenant on Economic Social and Cultural Rights (ICESCR), and the International Covenant on Civil and Political Rights (ICCPR) cite human dignity as the foundation of the human rights regime. Generally, the concept of human dignity ensures autonomy for an individual to make decisions on matters affecting them. It therefore flows that an individual's sexual autonomy protects their freedom to choose when and with whom to engage in sexual intercourse.[127]

However, in order to protect individual freedoms, the concept of sexual autonomy cannot function unrestrained.[128] If one were simply able to engage in sexual intercourse with whomever one chooses, it

123 Bronitt and McSherry (n 4) 638.

124 Amnesty International, 'Rape and Sexual Violence' (2011) *Human Rights Law and Standards in the International Criminal Court* (Report, 2 March 2021) www.amnesty.org/en/documents/IOR53/001/2011/en/.

125 *R v Kitchener* (1993) 29 NSWLR 696, 697 (Kirby P).

126 Maria Eriksson, *Defining Rape Emerging Obligations for States under International Law?* (Martinus Nijhoff, 2011) 8.

127 Jack Vidler, 'Ostensible Consent and the Limits of Sexual Autonomy' (2017) 17 *Macquarie Law Journal* 103, 109.

128 Ibid 110.

could infringe on another's autonomy if they did not consent to such acts. Accordingly, the law does not assure unlimited sexual access to an individual, but rather aims to protect negative sexual autonomy, being a freedom to control one's own sexuality and freedom from unwanted sexual access.[129] It is therefore the aim that sexual autonomy operates to promote the freedom to seek intimacy with a willing and informed partner.

Ultimately, an individual's right to sexual autonomy as an aspect of physical and mental integrity is a core human rights value protected by the criminalisation of sexual violence, and provides the basis for the legal concept of consent.[130] However, other human rights have also influenced the development of the legal concept of consent, including:

- The right to equality, which has influenced the abolishment of the marital rape immunity, implied consent and mistaken belief in consent and
- The right to privacy and respect for family life, which has influenced the abolishment of laws repressing prostitution and homosexuality, as well as liberalizing consensual sadomasochistic acts.[131]

The rights of equality and non-discrimination require that there should be equality in the weight placed on free and full agreement to sexual activity, for all parties involved.[132] When accompanied by threat, force or coercion, it is accepted that it is impossible for the victim to exercise their right to sexual autonomy.[133]

Despite the importance of recognising these rights within the scope of sexual autonomy, it is also important that rights are balanced with their counterparts – for example, the need to alter the 'veil of privacy' in order to protect the vulnerable has been increasingly acknowledged.[134] This is contrasted with the concern that the desire to preserve an individual's liberty and right to privacy could result in dangerous forms of sexual activity remaining beyond the ambit of the law.[135] This debate

129 Ibid 109.

130 Amnesty International (n 124) www.amnesty.org/en/documents/IOR53/001/2011/en/.

131 Bronitt and McSherry (n 4) 638.

132 Amnesty International (n 124) www.amnesty.org/en/documents/IOR53/001/2011/en/.

133 Ibid.

134 See, e.g., Bronitt and McSherry (n 4) 638; Simon Bronitt, 'The Right to Sexual Privacy, Sado-masochism and the Human Rights (Sexual Conduct) Act 1994 (Cth) (1995) 2(1) *Australian Journal of Human Rights* 59.

135 Bronitt, (n 134) 59.

has particularly arisen in the context of sadomasochism, being sexual activity that inflicts physical or mental suffering on another person who derives pleasure from the pain.[136] This will be discussed in more detail in Chapter 4.

In 1994, the House of Lords considered the specific issue of consent to bodily harm inflicted through sadomasochism in *R v Brown*.[137] The decision concerned a group of homosexual men who, for several years, had been engaging in sadomasochistic sexual acts including branding, caning, body piercing and bloodletting and so on. The activity came to the attention of the police and the men were charged and convicted of actual bodily harm under section 47 of the *Offences Against the Person Act 1861* (UK) and wounding under section 20.[138] The men appealed on the basis that the trial judge was incorrect in his exclusion of consent as a defence.

The House of Lords by a 3:2 majority dismissed the appeal. The majority ultimately held that consent cannot be raised as a defence to conduct that causes or is likely to cause actual bodily harm unless it was a foreseeable incident of lawful activity, for example, games, sports, lawful chastisement or correction and reasonable surgical interferences.[139] Lord Lowry considered that 'it is not in the public interest that people should try to cause or should cause, each other actual bodily harm for no good reason and that it is an assault if actual bodily harm is caused (except for good reason)'.[140] On the other hand, the minority judges were both reluctant to make a decision that would invade the privacy rights of the participants as they considered that the conduct was performed in private, therefore falling outside of the scope of the criminal law.[141]

The decision of *R v Brown* has been the subject of significant criticism for potentially undermining values of individual autonomy and concerns about 'unwarranted state intrusion into private matters'.[142] Others, however, endorse that violence should not be the subject of legal protection just because it occurs in private – and such a view could lead the way for more dangerous behaviour to be distorted under the guise of private consent.[143] Ultimately, it is evident that the continued

136 Ibid.
137 [1992] UKHL 7; [1993] 2 WLR 556.
138 Ibid.
139 Ibid.
140 Ibid 581–582.
141 Ibid.
142 Bronitt (n 134) 59.
143 Ibid.

development of consent laws requires careful consideration and balance of all human rights.

Law reform

Most common law countries, including Canada, New Zealand, England, parts of Australian and the United States, have extensively reformed their laws surrounding sexual offences over the last 20–30 years.[144] It is considered that there were three significant waves of reform to the laws of consent among common law countries.[145]

The first wave of reform began in the United States in the 1970s. Further reform followed in the 1980s in New South Wales, Canada and New Zealand, and then in the 2000s in England, Wales, Scotland, South Africa, New South Wales, Victoria and South Australia.[146]

In most of these jurisdictions, each wave represented the development of three key reforms: (1) a statutory definition of consent; (2) an objective test for determining the defendant's state of mind (*mens rea*); and (3) a list of evidential and conclusive presumptions about consent and circumstances that vitiate consent.[147]

Several factors contributed towards the amendment of the laws pertaining to sexual offences during this time, including increased awareness about sexual violence and the treatment of complainants within the legal system.[148] A highly persuasive factor in prompting significant reform were the feminist movements that occurred across Western states during the 1960s and 1970s.

Feminists promoted reform largely by highlighting the inadequacies and discriminatory nature of substantive laws and procedures dealing with sexual offences,[149] for example, the treatment of rape victims during cross-examination and the development of rape shield laws. Moreover, it was commonly posited that the laws governing consent legitimised dangerous stereotypes about female sexuality such as 'no' means 'yes' and that women are '(typically) sexually masochistic'.[150]

144 Vidler (n 127) 103, 105.
145 Annie Cossins, 'Why Her Behaviour Is Still on Trial: The Absence of Context in the Modernisation of The Substantive Law on Consent' (2019) 42(2) *UNSW Law Journal* 462, 465.
146 Ibid 465.
147 Ibid 466.
148 Australian Law Reform Commission (ALRC), *Family Violence – A National Legal Response,* Report No 114 (2010) 1111.
149 Bronitt and McSherry (n 4) 754.
150 Ibid 710.

The 1970s women's movement aimed at liberalising the widespread public attitudes regarding sexuality and at liberating the individual's natural approach to sexuality, resulting in increased gender equality.[151] Feminists and reformers argued that criminal laws prohibiting rape often displayed a cultural expectation of proper female behaviour.

It was proposed that crimes that only condemn sexual violence accompanied by force actually enhanced opportunities for coercive sex. Ultimately, the feminist viewpoint of rape contributed towards changing the focus away from the behavior or conduct of the victim, and instead onto the conduct of the accused.[152]

Whilst feminism continues to play an influential role in promoting further legal reform to our sexual offence laws, liberalism and individual rights of autonomy and principles of privacy (as discussed above) have also influenced the contemporary construction of consent laws.[153]

Australia

Feminist and political groups have advocated successfully over the past several decades for reform to each state and territory's consent laws in Australia. These groups have advocated for ongoing Commonwealth and state government policy concerning prevention, support, education and legislative changes pertaining to rape. For instance, since the mid-1980s the Commonwealth government has had a policy unit, currently the Office for Women, along with other initiatives that focus solely on rape and reform.

The first significant reform in Australia occurred in New South Wales in 1981 when the government introduced the *Crimes (Sexual Assault) Amendment Act 1981* (NSW).[154] This reform was prompted by extensive consultation with feminist activist groups who were active in advocating for greater recognition of sexual offences in the preceding decades.[155] For example, the first Rape Crisis Centre in Australia was opened in Sydney in 1974.[156]

151 Patricia Donat and John D'Emilio, 'A Feminist Redefinition of Rape and Sexual Assault: Historical Foundations and Change' (1992) 48 (1) *Journal of Social Issues* 9.

152 Ibid.

153 Bronitt and McSherry (n 4) 754.

154 The rules governing consent and the fault element operated to entrench and legitimate dangerous stereotypes about female sexuality in rethinking rape law.

155 Peter Rush, 'Criminal Law and the Reformation of Rape in Australia' in Clare McGlynn and Vanessa E. Munro (eds), *Rethinking Rape Law: International and Comparative Perspectives* (Taylor & Francis Group) 237, 239.

156 Ibid.

Feminists group advocated that sexual assault was an instance of violence and the substantive law of rape should be amended to reflect this fact. Accordingly, the *Crimes (Sexual Assault) Amendment Act 1981* (NSW) created a definition of consent that reconstructed rape as the infliction of harm with intent to have sexual intercourse.[157] This initial wave of reform was therefore concerned with progressing an understanding of rape as a social and political problem of violence – particularly violence against women.

The 1990s signalled a second wave of legislative reform. These reforms were focused on registering the legal problem of rape in 'gender-neutral' terms.[158] This was achieved through a number of substantive amendments to the definition of rape, including the introduction of neutral terminology such as 'sexual penetration' and the expansion of penetration to include a breadth of bodily orifices, such as the anus or mouth.[159] This had the unintentional effect of assisting with the decriminalisation of homosexual acts in Australia.[160] The second wave of reform also saw the development of the standard of consent, which began to be included in definitions of sexual offences.[161]

The third and most recent period of reform was phrased in terms of public health and human rights, that is, through the language of the 'rights of the victim' and the sexual autonomy of individuals.[162] For example, most recent reform of sexual offences in Victoria is phrased to 'uphold the fundamental right of every person to make decisions about his or her sexual behaviour and to choose not to engage in sexual activity'.[163] This wave also saw the shift towards a communicative model of consent with a positive definition of consent, which was endorsed by the Australian Law Reform Commission's report on family violence in 2010.[164] Consent laws now focus on a victim's 'free agreement', with variations among jurisdictions.

All Australian jurisdictions have now enacted a statutory definition of consent which focuses on 'free agreement', 'free and voluntary agreement' or 'consent freely and voluntarily given'.[165] Most recently,

157 *Crimes (Sexual Assault) Amendment Act 1981* (NSW); Rush (n 155) 237, 238.
158 Rush (n 155) 237, 239.
159 Ibid 239.
160 Ibid.
161 Ibid 240.
162 Ibid.
163 ALRC (n 148) 67.
164 Ibid.
165 See s 36 *Crimes Act 1958* (Vic), s 2A(1) *Criminal Code* (Tas), s 61HE(2) *Crimes Act 1900* (NSW), s 46(2) *Crimes Act 1935* (SA), s 192(2) *Criminal Code* (NT), s 348(1) *Criminal Code* (Qld), s 319(2) *Criminal Code* (WA).

the state of New South Wales has committed to adopting an affirmative consent model which requires a person to say or do something to affirm they have consented before sexual intercourse occurs.[166] In addition, an accused's belief in consent will not be reasonable unless they say or do something to ascertain consent.

United Kingdom

The law in the United Kingdom provided the basis for many American and Australian statutes. The term 'rape' originally referred to the non-consensual crime of violent theft (from the Latin *raptus* or *rapere*).

During the 1970s, the decision of *DPP v Morgan* was considered to be one of the triggers of the second wave of feminist activism in relation to rape laws.[167] This case considered that a man could not be found guilty of rape if he had an honest (even if unreasonable) belief that the woman was consenting.[168] *Morgan* confirmed feminist concerns that the legal system was not designed to treat female complainants fairly.[169]

The outrage associated with the *Morgan* judgement pushed the government to establish an advisory committee to review the laws surrounding rape in England.[170] This ultimately resulted in the establishment of *Sexual Offences (Amendment) Act 1976* (UK). While the 1976 Act did not abolish the decision of *Morgan*, it did respond to other feminist concerns, namely the misuse of sexual history evidence in rape trials.[171] Despite the reforms implemented by the 1976 Act, complainants continued to face scrutiny before the courts as rape myths were commonly cited. For example, McGlynn (2011) cites a case where a female complainant was held to be guilty of contributory negligence due to her actions of accepting a lift from the rapist.[172]

Feminist critique during the 1980s and 1990s highlighted injustices with the police, judiciary and other aspects of the legal system and

166 NSW Government, 'Consent Law Reform' *Communities and Justice* (Media Release, 25 May 2021) www.dcj.nsw.gov.au/news-and-media/media-releases/consent-law-reform.

167 *DPP v Morgan* [1975] 2 WLR 913; Clare McGlynn, 'Feminist Activism and Rape Law Reform in England and Wales' in Clare McGlynn and Vanessa E. Munro (eds), *Rethinking Rape Law: International and Comparative Perspectives* (Taylor & Francis Group) 139, 139.

168 Ibid.

169 Ibid.

170 Ibid 140.

171 Ibid.

172 Ibid.

prompted protests for change.[173] Notable reforms over time of course included the possibility that a husband could be guilty of raping his wife (*R v R* [1992] 1 AC 599), the 1994 Criminal Justice Public Order Act's recognition that men could also be victims of rape, as well as the removal of the requirement for judges to warn juries against convicting on the uncorroborated evidence of a woman.[174]

Ongoing feminist critique led to the United Kingdom Home Offices Sex Offences Review (1999) which intended to review the law pertaining to sex offences.[175] The findings of this review were subsequently published in the *Setting the Boundaries* report in 2000.

This report recommended that consent should be defined as 'free agreement' and that the definition should include a list of situations in which consent is deemed not to be present.[176] These recommendations took form in the current *Sex Offences Act 2003* (UK).[177]

The mid-nineteenth-century shift to the 'without consent' model in the United Kingdom reflected the modernising influence of liberal values on the criminal law and developments in 'Enlightenment philosophy'.[178] Until the introduction of the current *Sex Offences Act 2003* (UK), the common law governed the meaning of consent in England. It was the landmark case of *R v Olugboja* in 2003 that set the law of consent in a new direction.[179] In this case, the English Court of Appeal endorsed an 'ordinary meaning' approach in determining consent. The Court held that consent is a question of fact to be determined by the jury and that the jury will usually need to be directed to adopt an 'ordinary meaning' approach of consent for the purposes of determining rape.[180] That is, the Court considered that the jury should be directed to:

> concentrate on the state of mind of the victim immediately before the act of sexual intercourse, having regard to all the relevant circumstances; and in particular, the events leading up to the act and her reaction to them showing their impact on her mind.[181]

173 Ibid.
174 Ibid.
175 Vidler (n 127) 103, 105.
176 Ibid 106.
177 *Sex Offences Act 2003* (UK).
178 Bronitt and McSherry (n 4) 657.
179 *Sex Offences Act 2003* (UK); *R v Olugboja* [1982] QB 320.
180 Bronitt and McSherry (n 4) 657.
181 *R v Olugboja* [1982] QB 320, 332.

This ordinary meaning approach permits the jury to examine and scrutinise the quality of consent in each individual case with regard to the capacity of the victim. This allows the jury to consider modern, less traditional factors known to vitiate consent such as fraud or abuse of power.

However, one of the problems with this approach to determining consent is that the concept of consent, and circumstances that vitiate consent, are by no means a settled standard within the community.[182] This invites inconsistency in approach. Moreover, by inviting the jury to apply the 'ordinary meaning' of consent, it is considered that juries are effectively left to legislate the 'boundaries of rape' in each particular case.[183] While this is aimed at reflecting community standards of acceptable sexual behaviour, often in favour of the complainant, providing such autonomy to the jury also provides the opportunity for rape myths and other stereotypes to be applied unchallenged.[184]

The absence of an accepted definition of consent also enables jury directions to be similarly problematic. By way of example, in the case of *R v John,* Bollen J directed the jury that there was nothing wrong with a husband using 'rougher than usual handling' to overcome a wife's initial resistance.[185]

While much work has been done on redefining consent to meet modern expectations, the United Kingdom retains some aspects of ancient law in this regard. One such example is maintaining the distinction between the offence of rape (by penile penetration) and assault by penetration (using any part of the body or object).

United States of America

The first American rape statutes were influenced by the English common law definition of rape as 'illicit carnal knowledge of a female by force against her will'. From its initial independence in 1776 until the late nineteenth century, the United States imported the English definition of rape as carnal knowledge.[186] Similar to those seen in the United Kingdom, rape law also required that the victim provide the utmost resistance, chastity and to make their complaint promptly.[187] Over time,

182 Bronitt and McSherry (n 4) 667.

183 Ibid.

184 Ibid.

185 *R v Johns* (Supreme Court of South Australia, Bollen J, 26 August 1992) 12–13.

186 Donald Dripps, 'Rape, Law and American Society' in Clare McGlynn and Vanessa E. Munro (eds), (Taylor & Francis Group) 224, 226.

187 Ibid.

the courts modified the resistance requirement to be that only reasonable resistance was required; otherwise, most legal statutes were based on this common law definition until the mid-1900s.[188]

By the 1800s, feminists were extensively campaigning for change to the laws regarding sexual violence, especially in respect of race.[189] At this point in time in American society, rape was considered to be a crime committed against the chastity of a white woman, particularly when perpetrated by a black male stranger.[190]

While the extent of reform in the United States in more recent decades has varied from state to state, generally, Lyon (2004) considers there were two major categories of reform: (1) progress towards the elimination of the marital rape exemption and (2) defining rape in terms of the non-consent of the victim rather than the force of an attacker.[191] Feminists also continued during this time to campaign for the recognition that white defendants (without the requirement of being strangers or violent to their victims) should be able to be prosecuted.[192] This followed the recognition that stereotyping rapists had particularly harmful effects on African American men.[193]

The second half of the twentieth century signalled a series of reforms to rape laws, beginning with the proposed definition of rape in the MPC.[194] The MPC was drafted by the America Law Institute in 1962. The MPC rape provisions provided that:

> A male who has sexual intercourse with a female not his wife is guilty of rape if: (a) he compels her to submit by force or by threat of imminent death, serious bodily injury, extreme pain or kidnapping, to be inflicted on anyone; or (b) he has substantially impaired her power to appraise or control her conduct by administering or employing without her knowledge drugs, intoxicants or other means for the purpose of preventing resistance; or (c) the female is unconscious; or (d) the female is less than 10 years old. Section (a) still requires penetration, force, and the absence of consent.[195]

188 Ibid.
189 Estelle B. Freedman, *Redefining Rape: Sexual Violence in the Era of Suffrage and Segregation* (Harvard University Press, 2013) 34.
190 Ibid.
191 Lyon (n 22) 277, 282.
192 Freedman (n 189) 34.
193 Ibid.
194 Ibid.
195 *Model Penal Code* § 213.1 (1980).

Under the MPC, rape is not a felony of the first degree as there is no serious bodily harm if the victim was a 'voluntary social companion' and had previously engaged in sexual liberties.[196] The MPC also includes requirements of resistance by the victim, the reporting of crimes within three months and corroboration of the victim's testimony.[197]

The MPC definition of rape was therefore only a conservative revision of the common law statute.[198] It only sought to marginally expand the definition of rape and made minor reductions to the burden of proving resistance.[199] Moreover, it continued to perpetuate existing rape myths by allowing the use of a victim's sexual past as relevant evidence.

The MPC was used as a foundation for the criminal codes in two-thirds of American states, while the rest of the states retained the English common law concept of consent. In 1961, Illinois became the first US state to adopt a comprehensive criminal code based on the MPC.[200]

The MPC led a wave of reform that arose from the prevalent feminist movement of the 1970s and has continued to the present day (known as the 'rape reform movement' or 'anti-sexual assault revolution').[201] Following concerns about increased offending and outdated ideals, reformers and feminists lobbied to revise the legal definition and criminal procedure pertaining to rape.[202]

Reform in the 1970s and 1980s resulted in a number of US jurisdictions amending statutes to repeal prejudicial criminal procedures, including the requirement of proving resistance.[203] These efforts resulted in pronounced developments in sexual assault legislation, and rape statutes in each state were redrafted, resulting in not a 'single set of rape laws or a single system for enforcement, but instead 51 different rape statutes and 51 different procedural systems'.[204] The aims that guided these reforms were a desire to: redefine the offense of rape, alter and improve the evidentiary rules, regulate the statutory age of consent and create a penalty structure.[205]

196 *Model Penal Code* § 213.1 (1980).
197 *Model Penal Code* §§ 213.1, 213.6 (1980).
198 Gillespie and King (n 13) 15, 17.
199 Ibid.
200 Dripps (n 186) 224, 226.
201 Gillespie and King (n 13) 15, 15; Lyon (n 22) 277, 282.
202 Ibid 17.
203 Dripps (n 186) 224, 227.
204 Ibid 224.
205 Gillespie and King (n 13) 15, 18.

Consent elsewhere – case study

Rape reform and the conceptualisation of consent have varied markedly among jurisdictions. In some jurisdictions the notion of consent – and consent laws – has progressed with significant variance. This is often reflective of varying attitudes towards women and sex crimes and also contributes to the interplay between legal systems of secular and non-secular law. While many common law jurisdictions now view consent as 'free agreement' between parties, other jurisdictions still possess definitions of rape that reflect the common law positions outlined above.

Two examples are examined below.

Nigeria

Since its independence in 1960, family and personal matters in Nigeria have been governed by three systems of law: general, Muslim and customary laws. Under Nigerian law, rape is defined as forcible unlawful sexual intercourse, without a women's consent.[206]

Section 357 of the *Criminal Code* states:

> Any person who has unlawful carnal knowledge of a woman or girl without her consent, or with her consent, if consent is obtained by force or by means of threat or intimidation of any kind, or by fear of harm, or by any means of false and fraudulent representation as to the nature of the act, or in the case of a married woman, by personating her husband, is guilty of an offense which is called rape.[207]

Section 282(1) of the *Penal Code* states that:

> A man is said to commit rape if he has sexual intercourse with a woman in any of the following circumstances – (a) against her will; (b) without her consent; (c) with her consent, when her consent has been obtained by putting her in fear of death or hurt; (d) with her consent, when the man knows that he is not her husband and that her consent is given because she believes that he is another man to whom she is or believes herself to be lawfully married; (e) with or

206 Chineze J. Onyejekwe, 'Nigeria: The Dominance of Rape' (2008) 10(1) *Journal of International Women's Studies* 48, 52.

207 *Federal Republic of Nigeria Criminal Code Act* s 357.

without her consent, when she is under fourteen years of age or of unsound mind'.[208]

The two Codes have virtually the same effect, both notably limiting perpetrators of rape to men, and victims as women.[209] Evidently, the offence of rape under the Codes adopts a position that is akin to the common law definition of rape as carnal knowledge. Under the Codes, a man cannot be guilty of raping his wife, a position that is in keeping with the sociocultural perception that forced sexual intercourse within a marriage does not constitute rape (as seen in the historical marital rape immunity discussed above).[210] The Codes also do not recognise penetration of other female bodily orifices, including the anus or mouth.[211]

In 2015, the *Violence Against Persons Prohibition Act* (VAPP) came into force which is now the primary legislation for mandating various forms of sexual violence, including rape.[212] The VAPP displaces the Codes in respect of rape and other sexual offences.[213] Under the VAPP, both men and women are recognised as perpetrators of rape and are capable of being raped themselves.[214] The VAPP clarifies that a person can be raped through the vagina, anus or mouth and that the rape may occur with an object. Quite significantly, the VAPP also recognises both marital rape and gang rape.[215] A person convicted of rape under the VAPP is liable to the sentence of life imprisonment.[216]

According to academics, the Nigerian laws pertaining to rape are outdated and do not adequately specify the conditions around sexual consent and how it should be obtained.[217] Under these laws, it is on victims to prove the absence of consent. Moreover, procedural and evidential requirements impede the process with impossibly difficult standards.[218] For example, corroborative evidence is required to

208 *Federal Republic of Nigeria Penal Code (Northern States) Federal Provisions* Act s 282(1).
209 Akintayo Olamide Ogunwale, 'A Review of the Conceptual Issues, Social Epidemiology, Prevention and Control Efforts Relating to Rape in Nigeria' (2019) 23(4) *African Journal of Reproductive Health* 108, 111.
210 Ibid.
211 Ibid.
212 Ibid; *Violence Against Persons (Prohibition) Act* (2015).
213 Ogunwale (n 209) 108, 112.
214 Ibid; *Violence Against Persons (Prohibition) Act* (2015).
215 Ogunwale (n 209) 108, 112.
216 Ibid 112.
217 Ibid 116.
218 Ibid.

'confirm, support and strengthen' other pieces of evidence, and circumstantial evidence is not accepted by the courts.[219]

Sharia law and Sharia courts are increasingly recognised within Nigeria, and Sharia criminal codes operate in 12 of Nigeria's 36 states.[220] These laws detail *Hadd* offences, which are offences with specific punishments mentioned in the Koran (although Sharia penal codes also include punishments not mentioned in the Koran such as stoning and death).[221]

Within Sharia penal codes, rape is treated as a form of *zena* (or *zina*), being illicit sexual intercourse.[222] *Zena* is described as a sin that Allah will punish directly, except where there is a confession to atone for the act.[223] Reporting rape is the equivalent to confessing to *zena* and unless accompanied by the testimony of two witnesses or a confession from the rapist, rape is almost impossible to prove.[224] Accordingly, women find themselves liable for *zena* punishments. Therefore, it is commonly cited that Sharia penal codes deprive women of protection from rape and sexual assaults.[225]

Iran

There is limited statistical or academic information surrounding rape in Iran.[226] No official statistics have been published detailing the number of reported rape and sexual assault crimes, or related subsequent conviction rates.[227] According to Aghtaie (2017), this is reflective of the fact that 'violence against women is not understood as an issue of gender inequality by the Iranian government, and the protection of women from violence is not a government priority'.[228]

219 Ibid.

220 Ayesha Imam, *Wilson Center*, 'Women, Muslim Laws and Human Rights in Nigeria' (Publication, 2003) www.wilsoncenter.org/publication/women-muslim-laws-and-human-rights-nigeria.

221 Ibid.

222 Onyejekwe (n 206) 48, 53.

223 Ogunwale (n 209) 108, 114.

224 Imam (n 220).

225 Ibid.

226 Nadia Aghtaie, 'Breaking the Silence: Rape Law in Iran and Controlling Women's Sexuality' in Nicole Westmarland and Geentanjali Gangoli (eds), *International Approaches to Rape* (Policy Press, 2011) 121, 123.

227 Ibid.

228 Nadia Aghtaie, 'Rape within Heterosexual Intimate Relationships in Iran: Legal Frameworks, Cultural and Structural Violence' (2017) 6(2) *Families, Relationships and Societies* 167.

Following the Iranian revolution in 1979, Iran emerged as an Islamic state with Sharia law being declared as the law of the land.[229] As an Islamic state, the Guardian Council is responsible for approving bills passed by Parliament and the Council can veto any bills that it considers to be inconsistent with its internal laws.[230]

According to Aghtaie (2011), there is no word in the Iranian dictionary that means rape.[231] A combination of two words, *ajovoz jensi* or *taroz jensi*, which mean sexual attack or sexual harassment, are used as synonyms for 'rape'.[232]

Sex outside of marriage is dealt with under Article 82 of the Iranian Penal Code and is punishable by *Hadd* (as described above).[233] Rape is referred to as *zen-r ba onf va ekrah* (adultery with force and duress) and falls under the category of *zena* (as described above).[234] *Zena-e ba onf va ekrah* under Iranian law means forced sexual intercourse with a woman to whom the accuser is married.[235] Under this offence, penile penetration can be of the vagina or anus and does not extend to instances of forced oral sex.[236]

According to Article 82 of the Iranian penal code, the punishment for *zena* (sex outside of marriage) can be the death penalty.[237]

As a rape is a subsection of *zena*, women who report rape are co-defendants as well as complainants due to the fact that sex outside of marriage is illegal.[238] Aghtaie (2017) also predicts that courts will more likely than not consider that the sexual encounters were consensual as there should be no reason for a woman to be in the residence of a man who is a stranger.[239]

Zena can be proved in court in the following circumstances: confession before a judge (Article 68);[240] on the testimony of four men, or three just men and two just women in cases where the designated punishment is either stoning or flogging (Article 74); or on the testimony of two just men and four just women in cases where the designated punishment is

229 Aghtaie (n 226) 168.
230 Ibid 121.
231 Ibid 125.
232 Ibid.
233 Aghtaie (n 228) 167, 171.
234 Ibid.
235 Aghtaie (n 226) 121, 127.
236 Ibid.
237 Aghtaie (n 228) 167, 171.
238 Ibid.
239 Ibid.
240 Aghtaie (n 226) 121, 127.

flogging (Article 75).[241] The testimony of women alone or in conjunction with the testimony of only one man cannot be used to prove *zena*; instead, it can be regarded as *Qazf* (false accusation), which creates a separate liability for punishment (Article 76).[242] A judge can use his own knowledge to prove *zena*; however, the judge must make the source of his knowledge transparent (Article 105).[243] This 'knowledge' is by no means uniform in practice, creating the further issue of inconsistency.[244]

It is common in Iran that rape victims are blamed for provoking the incident, and even where the perpetrator is charged with a crime, the victim is still shamed.[245] An example of how rape trials are handled can be evidenced by the 1999 Supreme Court case concerning a complaint by a 24-year-old woman, Kolsum, of rape by three men.[246] Kolsum was lost in the city when a man approached her and took her to his friend's place.[247] Kolsum was told to pretend to be the man's sister, and the man's wife put make-up on Kolsum and cut her hair.[248] Kolsum was then taken to another house and raped by three men at knifepoint.

During the trial, Kolsum was asked by one of the judges whether she enjoyed having sex with the defendants.[249] It was ultimately argued (and accepted) that the fact that Kolsum was wearing make-up was an indicator of her willingness to have sex with the defendants.[250] It was also stated that Kolsum had several opportunities to get away, yet she failed to do so.[251]

The legislative shortcomings combined with the gender discrimination severely limit the ability of victims of Iran to report the crime of rape to police, and even when reported, it is difficult to prove rape crimes under the *Iranian Penal Code* and to provide the number of witnesses required.[252] Moreover, it is possible for perpetrators to avoid punishment by denying their crime after confession or by repenting prior to testimony (Article 81).[253]

241 Ibid 128.
242 Ibid.
243 Ibid.
244 Ibid.
245 Ibid 124.
246 Ibid 128; 'Mozakerat va ara-e heyat-e omumi' [Negotiations and votes of the Supreme Court] (1378/1991) divan-e ali-e keshvar (the Supreme Court).
247 Aghtaie (n 226) 121, 128.
248 Ibid.
249 Ibid.
250 Ibid.
251 Ibid.
252 Ibid 136.
253 Ibid 131.

According to Aghtaie (2011), it is clear that the Iranian legal system maintains some of the historical views described above – being that the 'virginity of an unmarried woman [is] a signifier of her chastity, and losing her virginity outside marriage is perceived as a colossal disaster for both her and her family'.[254] These ideals are considered to directly impact the low rates of reporting and difficulties with achieving rape prosecutions.[255]

Rape myths and consent today

Rape laws have developed over time to be understood first as a property offence, and then to the current construction as the absence of consent or 'free agreement' between parties.

Despite such reform, the common law legacies and historical constructions of consent described in this chapter have promoted prejudicial rape myths that lawmakers have not easily departed from. Consequently, statements such as British Judge Lord Matthew Hale's 1600s proposition that rape is 'an accusation easily to be made and hard to be proved and harder to be defended by the party accused tho never so innocent' find themselves outdated, yet still relevant, centuries later.[256]

As the legal concepts of consent have developed over the centuries, many rape myths continue to influence society, including the courts and police. The historical view of rape as a property crime has continued to promote the belief that women lie about being raped.[257] For example, in the twelfth century a law entitled 'an Appeal concerning the Rape of Virgins' required a report of rape to be made shortly after an assault took place, and the victim was required to present her torn or blood-stained clothes.[258] The victim would also have to her body examined by law-abiding women who would attest to whether she was a virgin or not and as to whether she had been raped.'[259] It was not until the late 1200s that the virginity of the victim was no longer considered relevant to proving the offence or to the consideration of the applicable punishment.[260]

Rape myths have greatly influenced the investigation and prosecution of rape offences. Accordingly, statutes were enacted with a view to

254 Ibid 140.
255 Ibid.
256 ALRC (n 148) 1112.
257 Tracy et al (n 2) 5.
258 MacFarlane (n 15).
259 Ibid.
260 Ibid.

protecting men's interests and led to a number of procedural issues that are considered to be prevalent today, for example, the requirement that a victim make a prompt complaint, the requirement of corroboration of a victim's testimony, the allowing of information regarding the victim's past sexual encounters to be admitted into evidence and allowing cautionary instructions that discredited victims to jurors.[261] Moreover, the unease around false rape allegations influenced the development of rape laws to include the requirement of physical force or violence to overpower a victim's resistance.[262]

Despite reform requiring 'free agreement', a continuum therefore remains perpetuating rape myths and promoting an understanding that 'real' rape only exists where it is perpetrated by a stranger, where it involves physical force or resistance and where it is reported immediately. At the other end of the spectrum, there is the less legitimate assault involving partners, non-physical coercion and delayed victim reporting. Accordingly, there is a common misconception that women are prone to fabricating allegations of sexual offence that continues to influence courtrooms and lawmakers.

261 Tracy et al (n 2) 5.
262 Ibid.

2 Consent as a modern construction?

The meaning of consent in a legal context

In criminalising sexual offences, society, through Parliament, seeks to prosecute those who have knowingly touched or penetrated another without consent.[1] As discussed in Chapter 1, the meaning of consent in a legal context most commonly refers to the 'free and voluntary agreement' of a person to engage in a sexual act. However, it is important to note that each separate jurisdiction uniquely defines consent, either in legislation or as a result of cases that have gone through the courts. A person's capacity, or ability, to legally consent to sexual activity, will usually depend on a number of factors such as age, intoxication level, physical disability, vulnerability, fraud and level of consciousness. Autonomous adult individuals with capacity are deemed to be legally capable of providing consent,[2] with the act of consenting itself becoming the factor that separates legal from illegal sexual interaction.[3]

The legal requirement that a person must provide consent to engage in sexual intercourse also operates to protect a person's freedom to decide whether or not to engage in sexual intercourse, freely and voluntarily, based on the circumstances and conditions of a particular sexual act.[4] Consent assumes that individuals possess a physical power to decide when and how they engage in sexual activity with others. 'Consent' itself

1 Criminal Law Review, 'Victoria's New Sexual Offence Laws', Department of Justice and Regulation (Vic); Brianna Chesser and April Zahra 'Stealthing: A Criminal Offence?' (2019) 31(2) *Current Issues in Criminal Justice* 217, 219.

2 Australian Law Reform Commission (ALRC), *Family Violence – A National Legal Response,* Report No 114 (2010) 1150.

3 Bianca Fileborn, Australian Institute of Family Studies, *Sexual Assault Laws in Australia* (ACSSA Resource Sheets) (2011) 7; Chesser and Zahra (n 1) 217, 219.

4 ALRC (n 2) 1150.

DOI: 10.4324/9781003165606-2

should therefore be a reflective, determined and unencumbered exertion of power that is free from fraud, duress or any threat of violence.

Consent in Australia

Australia is a common law country that bases its law system on the bicameral and adversarial legal system of the United Kingdom. Australia is divided into six states (New South Wales ('NSW'), Queensland, South Australia ('SA'), Tasmania, Victoria, Western Australia ('WA')) and two territories (Australian Capital Territory ('ACT') and Northern Territory ('NT')). In Australia, consent to sexual intercourse is governed by the common law and various criminal law statutes in each state and territory. Legislative material such as the *Crimes Act 1958* (Vic) outline the different types of circumstances that can occur where consent may not have been given.[5] The definition of consent under s 36 of the *Victorian Crimes Act* is based on the principle of free agreement, and any sexual activity between persons which lacks consent is an offence under the *Crimes Act*.[6] A lack of consent to sexual intercourse should attract criminal liability regardless of the age of the participants. The relevant offences which are linked to sexual activity without consent include rape and sexual assault. Rape is an offence (such as under s 38 of the *Victorian Crimes Act*) and sexual assault is an offence (such as under s 40 of the *Victorian Crimes Act*).[7] Each jurisdiction in Australia has a different sentence for the crime, ranging from 12 years' imprisonment to life imprisonment.[8]

All Australian jurisdictions have adopted legislative provisions governing the law pertaining to sexual offences. All Australian jurisdictions have their own set of substantive and procedural criminal laws, each differing in its reliance on, and compliance with, the common law.

Meaning of sexual intercourse/penetration

The offence of rape in all states and territories in Australia requires sexual penetration of some form. Most jurisdictions now adopt an all-encompassing definition of sexual acts.[9] Penetrative sexual offences

5 *Crimes Act 1958* (Vic).

6 Ibid s 36.

7 Ibid s 38, 40.

8 See, e.g., *Crimes Act 1900* (ACT) s 54(1); *Criminal Code 1899* (Qld) s 349(1).

9 See, e.g., *Crimes Act 1958* (Vic) s 35A; *Crimes Act 1900* (NSW) s 61H; *Crimes Act 1935* (SA) s 5; *Criminal Code* (WA) s 319; *Criminal Code* (Qld) s 347; *Criminal Code* (Tas) s 1; *Criminal Code* (NT) s 1.

are no longer gender-specific and include penetration by a penis, other body parts, and foreign objects. Furthermore, penetration is no longer limited to only the vagina and includes the penetration of any genitalia (including surgically constructed vaginas), the mouth, or any part of the body.[10] Most jurisdictions also prohibit a person from partaking in sexual penetration of themselves, another person, or an animal.[11]

Statutory definition of consent

The physical element of the offence, or the *actus reus*, requires the prosecution to prove that the sexual penetration occurred without consent.[12] All states in Australia, except the ACT, have a statutory definition of consent designed to provide legal clarity about when an individual is consenting to sexual contact.[13] These statutory definitions of consent are based on: free agreement,[14] free and voluntary agreement,[15] or consent freely and voluntary given.[16] 'Agreement' supports the notion that consent should be a positive state of mind and the word 'voluntary' ensures that only active engagement in sexual activity could be enough to constitute consent.[17] Unlike the common law understanding of consent, it is important to note that under statutes in Australia, overt resistance to the sexual act is not required.[18]

In most jurisdictions, it is an offence to continue to engage in sexual intercourse after the complainant has withdrawn their consent.[19] This amendment codified the decision in *Kaitamaki v The Queen*,[20] where the Privy Council held that 'sexual intercourse is a continuing act which only ends with withdrawal'.[21] In this case, the accused was charged with

10 Ibid.
11 *Crimes Act 1958* (Vic) s 39
12 Chesser and Zahra (n 1) 217, 221.
13 Ibid.
14 *Crimes Act 1958* (Vic) s 36; *Criminal Code* (Tas) s 2A(1).
15 *Crimes Act 1900* (NSW) s 61HA; *Crimes Act 1935* (SA) s 46(2); *Criminal Code* (NT) s 192(1).
16 *Criminal Code* (Qld) s 348(1); *Criminal Code* (WA) s 319(2).
17 Chesser and Zahra (n 1) 217, 221.
18 *Crimes Act 1900* (ACT) s 67(2); *Criminal Code* (NT) ss 192A(a)(b); *Crimes Act 1958* (Vic) s 36; *Criminal Code* (WA) s 319(2)(b); *Crimes Act 1900* (NSW) s 61HA(7); *Criminal Code* (Tas) s 2A.
19 *Crimes Act 1958* (Vic) s 36(2)(m); *Crimes Act 1900* (NSW) s 61H; *Crimes Act 1935* (SA) s 5; *Criminal Code* (WA) s 319; *Criminal Code* (Qld) s 347; *Criminal Code* (Tas) s 1; *Criminal Code* (NT) s 1; *Crimes Act 1935* (SA) s 5(1).
20 [1984] 2 All ER 435.
21 Ibid 253 (Lord Scarman).

breaking into the complainant's home and raping her twice. The accused argued that when he penetrated the complainant, he believed her to be consenting. However, when he became aware that the complainant was no longer consenting, he did not withdraw. It was held that whilst sexual intercourse occurs at the point of penetration, it is a continuing act that only ceases at the point of withdrawal.[22]

A case which sheds light on the importance of defining consent is *R v Wilkes and Briant* [1965].[23] The accused was on trial for rape and the main issue at hand was whether the complainant had consented to the sexual act. Her denial of consent was supported by other evidence; however, there were also substantial forms of evidence which showed consent by the complainant's conduct at the time. When instructing the jury, the trial judge focused on the principle that rape should be seen as: 'carnal knowledge of a female without her consent' as meaning 'without her free and conscious permission'.[24] A question raised by the jury was whether permission to engage in intercourse needed to be granted verbally, with the trial judge responding that permission need not be 'absolutely verbal'; rather, there needs to be a clear, free and conscious permission granted.[25] The accused was subsequently convicted of rape and then appealed.

On appeal, Smith J surmised that the trial judge's answer to the jury's question was both inadequate to deal with the situation and also unclear as to what should constitute consent.[26] The expression of 'free and conscious permission' was, in Smith J's view, likely to convey to the jury that though they need not look to words alone, something must be found in words before it could be held that consent had been given; or at least that some particular act equivalent to words was necessary.[27] Smith J concluded that in the trial judge's attempt at conveying the meaning of 'consent', he instead inadvertently confused the jury about the proper understanding of the concept of consent.[28] It was considered that the trial judge, instead of giving his somewhat ambiguous response to the question asked by the jury, should have restated the law on the issue of consent so as to make it abundantly clear that consent might be given by an act or by a course of conduct.[29] The appeal was allowed, and a new trial was ordered.

22 *Kaitamaki v The Queen [1984] 2 All ER 435.*
23 *R v Wilkes and Briant* [1965] VR 475.
24 Ibid.
25 Ibid.
26 *R v Wilkes and Briant* [1965] VR 475.
27 Ibid (Smith J).
28 Ibid (Smith J).
29 Ibid.

Circumstances where consent is vitiated

In each jurisdiction in Australia, legislation prescribes certain circumstances where consent to a sexual act evidently does not exist.[30] That is, despite the existence of a communicative model of consent, there are some cases that require further direction on consent.[31] If the prosecution can prove the presence of any of the circumstances as discussed below, the complainant's apparent consent is automatically deemed to be negated.[32] Most jurisdictions have codified or extended circumstances at common law where the complainant was not regarded as consenting.[33] The list is non-exhaustive, and in all other circumstances, consent follows the above definition of free and voluntary agreement.[34] In situations that fall outside of the exact scope of the listed circumstances, the common law is presumed to apply.

Vitiating consent through use of threat or force

All Australian jurisdictions stipulate that there is no consent where force is used or threatened to be used against the complainant. Most Australian jurisdictions specify that it must be the application of fear of force,[35] while others specify consent is not given where there is 'fear of bodily harm',[36] 'threats of terror',[37] or a 'reasonable fear of force'.[38] In SA, this threat may be express or implied.[39] The force or threatened force may be exerted against the complainant or against another person,[40] with only the ACT requiring the other person to be 'present or

30 *Crimes Act 1958* (Vic) s 36(2); *Criminal Code* (Qld) s 348(2); *Crimes Act* (SA) s 46(3); *Criminal Code Act* (Tas) s 2A(2); *Crimes Act* (NSW) s 61HA(2); *Criminal Code* (WA) s 319(2)(a); *Criminal Code* (NT) s 192(2).

31 Chesser and Zahra (n 1) 217, 223

32 Australia. Model Criminal Code Officers Committee (MCCOC) of the Standing Committee of Attorneys-General, Chapter 5 in *Model Criminal Code. Chapter 5, Sexual offences against the person: report* (The Committee, 1999) 41.

33 Ibid.

34 Ibid.

35 *Crimes Act 1900* (NSW) s 61HA(4)(c); *Crimes Act 1958* (Vic) s 36(2)(a); *Criminal Code* (Qld) s 348(2)(a); *Criminal Code* (WA) s 319(2)(a); *Crimes Act 1935* (SA) s 46(3)(a)(i); *Criminal Code* (Tas) 2A(2)(b); *Crimes Act 1900* (ACT) s 67(1)(a)–(c); *Criminal Code* (NT) s 192 (2)(a).

36 *Criminal Code* (Qld) s 348(2)(c).

37 *Crimes Act 1900* (NSW) s 61HA(4)(c).

38 *Criminal Code* (Tas) s 2A(2)(b).

39 *Crimes Act 1935* (SA) s 46(3)(a)(i).

40 *Crimes Act 1900* (NSW) s 61HA(4)(c); *Crimes Act 1958* (Vic) s 36(2)(a); *Criminal Code* (Qld) s 348(2)(a); *Criminal Code* (WA) s 319(2)(a); *Crimes Act 1935* (SA) s 46(3)(a)(i);

nearby'.[41] Some jurisdictions also specifically prescribe that there may be no consent where consent is obtained by intimidation,[42] coercion,[43] or extortion.[44]

In these circumstances, the jury must consider whether the nature of the threat and the degree of fear caused by the accused were sufficient to destroy the complainant's free and voluntary consent.[45] Violence or threats of violence have been held to vitiate consent in a variety of cases.[46] For example, in the Queensland case of *R v IA Shaw*,[47] the accused was driving the inebriated complainant home when the accused, who was older and stronger than the complainant, directed the complainant to a remote bushland, where he threatened her with a knife and had intercourse. The Court held that in these circumstances it was clearly open to the jury to determine that consent had been procured by means of intimidation.[48] Similarly, in the case of *R v Motlop,* the accused told the complainant that he would kill her and threatened her repeatedly with a knife.[49] The Queensland Court of Appeal emphasised that a gap in time between the threats and the intercourse did not preclude the jury from finding that the complainant had been intimidated into giving consent.[50] The Court of Appeal adopted a subjective test, clarifying that:

> The issue of consent is not determined by reference to the intention of the person inflicting the violence. The issue is whether consent was freely and voluntarily given by the complainant. That involves a consideration of whether consent of a particular complainant was obtained or induced by the conduct in question. The issue the jury has to determine, beyond reasonable doubt, was whether any consent by the complainant was obtained or induced by the earlier force or the threat or intimidation of further force should she not

Criminal Code (Tas) 2A(2)(b); *Crimes Act 1900* (ACT) s 67(1)(a)–(c); *Criminal Code* (NT) s 192 (2)(a).

41 *Crimes Act 1900* (ACT) s 67(1).

42 *Criminal Code* (Qld) s 348(2)(b); *Criminal Code* (WA) s 319(2)(a); *Crimes Act 1900* (NSW) s 61HA(6)(b).

43 *Crimes Act 1900* (NSW) s 61HA(6)(b).

44 *Crimes Act 1900* (ACT) s 67(1)(c).

45 Simon Bronitt, 'Rape and Lack of Consent' (1992) 16 *Criminal Law Journal* 289, 291.

46 See, e.g., *R v IA Shaw* [1996] 1 Qd R 641; *R v Motlop* [2013] QCA 30; *R v Moss* [2011] SASCFC 93; *R v Rajakaruna* [2004] VSCA 114; *R v Moss* [2011] SASCFC 93; *R v PS Shaw* [1995] 2 Qd R 97; *R v Parsons* [2000] QCA 136.

47 [1996] 1 Qd R 641.

48 Ibid.

49 *R v Motlop* [2013] QCA 30.

50 Ibid.

comply with the request for sexual intercourse. In determining that question, it was irrelevant whether another may *have ignored or* resisted a similar threat or what was the intention of the appellant at the time.[51]

Other Australian jurisdictions have reached similar findings. In the Victorian case of *R v Rajakaruna*,[52] the accused was convicted of multiple counts of rape against sex workers. In one instance, the accused refused the complainant's request for upfront payment, forced her into his car, and grabbed her neck while threatening to kill her. The Court of Appeal upheld the conviction of rape, finding sufficient evidence of threats and intimidation which compelled the complainant to have sexual intercourse without free and voluntary consent, notwithstanding that she may have consented in other circumstances.[53] A similar scenario was upheld in the South Australian Court of Appeal, where the complainant sex worker was threatened verbally and with a firearm.[54]

It is important to note, however, that the use of pressure that does not amount to coercion will not ultimately vitiate consent.

Non-physical threats

Some jurisdictions also recognise that there is no consent where it is obtained by non-physical or non-violent threats. SA specifies that there is no consent when it is obtained as a result of 'an express or implied threat to degrade, humiliate, disgrace or harass the person or another person'.[55] The ACT similarly lists threats to 'publicly humiliate, disgrace, physically or mentally harass'.[56] Other jurisdictions take a broader approach in prescribing that there is, or may be, no consent where there are threats 'that do not involve a threat of force',[57] 'fear of harm of any type'[58] or of 'any kind'.[59]

For example, in *R v Aiken*,[60] the accused persuaded the complainant that he was an undercover security guard who had witnessed her

51 Ibid.
52 *R v Rajakaruna* [2004] VSCA 114.
53 Ibid.
54 *R v Moss* [2011] SASCFC 93.
55 *Crimes Act 1935* (SA) s 46(3)(a)(ii).
56 *Crimes Act 1900* (ACT) s 67(1)(d).
57 *Crimes Act 1900* (NSW) s 61HA(6)(b).
58 *Crimes Act 1958* (Vic) s 36(2)(b); *Criminal Code* (NT) s 192(2)(a).
59 *Crimes Act 1900* (NSW) s 61HA(6)(b).
60 (2005) 63 NSWLR 719.

shoplifting, and that he would not report her if she performed sexual acts on him. The accused was convicted of sexual intercourse without consent.[61] On appeal, the conviction was quashed, as it was held that a non-violent threat did not vitiate consent for the purpose of the relevant legislative provisions at the time.[62] Importantly, NSW legislation has now been altered to recognise that non-violent threats may, in fact, negate consent.[63]

Asleep, unconscious, or affected by drugs or alcohol

Under legislation in most Australian jurisdictions, there is no consent when the complainant is asleep or unconscious.[64] Other jurisdictions specify being asleep or unconscious along with the effect of alcohol and other drugs. The common law similarly recognises that a complainant who is asleep may also be incapable of consenting.[65] In the case of *Banditt v The Queen*,[66] the accused broke into the complainant's house and commenced intercourse with her while she was asleep. The Court held that the complainant was not consenting, and the accused was reckless to the fact.[67] These directions were upheld on appeal.

In Victoria, SA, NSW, Tasmania, and the NT, a complainant will not be regarded as consenting to sexual conduct where they are so affected by alcohol or drugs that they are regarded as being 'incapable of freely agreeing' to the sexual activity.[68] In NSW, a person cannot consent to sexual intercourse while being 'substantially intoxicated by alcohol or any drug'.[69] The ACT prescribes a broader requirement, stating that a complainant will not have consented where the purported consent is caused by the effect of intoxicating liquor, drugs, or anaesthetic.[70] In *R v Blayney*,[71] the complainant was intoxicated to the point of requiring

61 Ibid.
62 Ibid [33] (Studdert J).
63 *Crimes Act 1900* (NSW) s 61HA(6)(b).
64 *Crimes Act 1900* (NSW) s 61HA(4)(b); *Crimes Act 1935* (SA) s 46(3)(c); *Crimes Act 1958* (Vic) s 36(2)(d); *Criminal Code* (Tas) s 2A(2)(h); *Criminal Code* (NT) s 192(2)(c).
65 *R v Mayers* (1872) 12 Cox CC 311.
66 (2005) 224 CLR 262.
67 Ibid [112].
68 *Crimes Act 1958* (Vic) s 36(2)(d); *Crimes Act 1935* (SA) s 46(3)(d); *Criminal Code* (Tas) s 2A(2)(h); *Criminal Code* (NT) s 192(2)(c); *Crimes Act 1900* (NSW) s 61HA(6)(a).
69 *Crimes Act 1900* (NSW) s 61HE(8)(a).
70 *Crimes Act 1900* (ACT) s 67(1)(e).
71 [2012] SASCFC 38.

physical assistance to walk to the accused's car. The complainant was unable to speak due to her intoxicated state. The accused and his brother had sexual intercourse with the complainant in the back seat. The Court held that the complainant was unable to consent.[72] In cases of ambiguity, whether the complainant was unconscious or intoxicated is a question of fact for the jury to determine.

Some academics view that the current law struggles to deal with the uncertainties inherent in establishing when a person is 'too intoxicated' to consent and consequently adopts an 'extreme' position. One of the alleged consequences of this position is that there is little distinction between 'prototypical drug-assisted rape' and more commonplace scenarios of drink spiking.[73]

Abuse of position of authority or trust

In Queensland, Tasmania, ACT, and NSW, there is no consent where the accused is in a position of authority or trust over the complainant.[74] In *Stubley v Western Australia*,[75] the accused had intercourse with a number of patients in his office over a period of years. The accused contended that consent was given in all cases. However, the complainants gave evidence that they were intimidated by his position of power and authority. The Court of Appeal accepted that intimidation by authority could be a factor in nullifying consent, such that consent would not be freely and voluntarily given.[76]

The courts have also accepted an abuse of authority as a factor of negating consent when the authority was false, as in the case of *Aiken* discussed above. Similarly, in *Michael v State of Western Australia*, the appellant impersonated a police officer and threatened to use coercive police powers against two sex workers if they did not comply with his sexual demands.[77] The complainants only acquiesced to sexual intercourse because they believed that the appellant was a police officer.

72 Ibid [26] (White J).

73 Emily Finch and Vanessa Munro, 'Intoxicated Consent and the Boundaries of Drug-Assisted Rape' (2003) *Criminal Law Review* 773, 774.

74 *Criminal Code* (Qld) s 348(2)(d); *Criminal Code* (Tas) s 2A(2)(e); *Crimes Act 1900* (ACT) s 67(1)(i); *Crimes Act 1900* (NSW) s 61HA(6)(c).

75 [2011] HCA 7.

76 Ibid.

77 *Michael v State of Western Australia* [2008] WASCA 66.

Unlawful detention

All jurisdictions except WA prescribe there is no consent where a person is unlawfully detained.[78]

Mistake and fraud

Consent is also vitiated where the complainant is mistaken about the sexual nature of the act, including where they have submitted because of false or fraudulent representations about the nature or purpose of the act.[79] These legislative provisions codify or extend the common law position as established in *Papadimitropoulos v The Queen*.[80] In this case, the accused procured a young woman to have sex with him by convincing her that they were married. The High Court held that the accused's conduct did not amount to rape.[81] The Court confirmed the earlier decision of *R v Clarence* that only certain forms of mistake or fraud could amount to rape, being where there was mistake about the identity of the person or about the fundamental nature of the act.[82] The law of consent has since been amended in various jurisdictions to incorporate the fraud recognised in *Papadimitropoulos.*[83]

R v Clarence

The effect of fraud on consent was unresolved until the 1988 case of R v Clarence.[84] The accused knowingly infected his wife with gonorrhoea and was accused of grievous bodily harm and assault occasioning actual bodily harm. The Court considered whether the wife's consent had been vitiated by the accused's failure to disclose the infection. Stephen J rejected the idea that fraud could vitiate consent in criminal matters, stating that 'if fraud vitiates consent, every case in which a man infects a woman or commits bigamy is also a case of rape'.[85] Stephen J considered that consent would only be vitiated where the fraud related

78 *Crimes Act 1900* (NSW) s 61HA(4)(d); *Crimes Act 1958* (Vic) s 36(2)(c); *Crimes Act 1935* (SA) s 46(3)(b); *Criminal Code* (Tas) s 2a(2)(d); *Crimes Act 1900* (ACT) s 67(1)(k); *Criminal Code* (NT) s 192(2(b).
79 *Papadimitropoulos v The Queen* (1957) 98 CLR 249.
80 Ibid.
81 Ibid.
82 (1889) 22 QB 23.
83 (1957) 98 CLR 249.
84 R v Clarence (1888) 22 QBD 23.
85 Ibid.

to 'the nature of the act itself, or as to the identity of the person who does the act'.[86] The Court therefore held that the husband could not be guilty of rape as the wife's consent was not obtained by fraud either as to the nature of the act or the identity of the accused.[87] The fact of the accused's infection did not alter the nature of the physical sexual act itself and the complainant's lack of knowledge was held to be immaterial to the issue of consent.[88]

High Court's decision in *Papadimitropoulos*

In *Papadimitropoulos*, the High Court confirmed the holding in *Clarence* that the mistake induced by fraud must relate to the 'nature and character of the act'. The High Court's decision was a unanimous joint judgement in which the judges adopted the view that the accused's conduct, did not constitute rape under Australian law. The judges preferred to emphasise and focus on the complainant's consent to the act based on the fact that there had not been any fraud or mistake as to the identity of the accused. The complainant at all material times, was aware of the identity of the accused, genuinely believed they were married, and so engaged in sexual intercourse with him on multiple occasions. The fact that he lied to the complainant about being legally married was not enough in order to constitute a rape conviction, and so the appeal by the accused was upheld by the High Court. A key point that the High Court had made in this instance, keeping with *Clarence*, was that only certain narrow forms of mistake or fraud could potentially form the basis of a rape conviction.[89] These were limited to mistake about the identity of a person's sexual partner or the fundamental nature of the act.[90] Crowe (2014) notes that it was not considered relevant that the complainant had thought she was engaging in marital intercourse as opposed to extra marital intercourse, considered that she was not ultimately decieved about the nature of the act itself.[91]

86 Ibid.
87 Ibid.
88 Ibid.
89 Jonathan Crowe, 'Fraud and Consent in Australian Rape Law' (2014) 38(4) *Criminal Law Journal* 236, 237.
90 Ibid.
91 Ibid.

Statute – mistake or fraud as to the sexual nature

In Victoria, SA, NSW, Tasmania, and the NT, consent is vitiated where the person agreed or submitted to the sexual activity because of fraudulent representations about the sexual nature of the act.[92] In some jurisdictions, this includes a mistaken belief that the sexual act is for medical or hygienic purposes.[93] These provisions codify the decisions of several common law cases. In the case of *R v Mobilio*,[94] the accused carried out internal vaginal examinations on several female patients using ultrasound transducers. These examinations were represented as being medically necessary but were solely for the accused's sexual gratification. The accused was convicted of rape. The most appropriate example of someone having provided consent to sexual intercourse based on a mistake as to the nature of the act can be seen in the case *R v Williams* [1925].[95] In this case, a singing teacher had told the victim that he needed to make an air passage to assist in her breathing which was to allegedly help her sing better. However, whilst the victim did consent to this, the defendant then engaged in sexual intercourse with the victim. The Court at first instance held that consent to the creation of the air passage was not consent to the actual act of sexual intercourse and that the victim had indeed been deceived as to the nature of the act proposed and thus any apparent consent had been negated.[96]

Identity fraud

In NSW, Victoria, Queensland, SA, and the NT, there is no consent where the complainant is mistaken about the identity of the person with whom they have engaged in sexual activity.[97] In *R v Pryor*,[98] the accused broke into the complainant's house with the intent to burgle her, and commenced sexual intercourse with the complainant as she slept. The complainant initially reciprocated the sexual advances under the

92 *Crimes Act 1958* (Vic) s 36(2)(h); *Crimes Act 1935* (SA) s 46(3)(h); *Criminal Code* (Tas) s 2A(g); *Criminal Code* (NT) s 192(2)(e); *Crimes Act 1900* (NSW) s 61HA(5).

93 *Crimes Act 1900* (NSW) s 61HA(5)(c); *Crimes Act 1958* (Vic) s 36(2)(j); *Criminal Code* (NT) s 192(1)(f).

94 [1991] VR 339.

95 *R v Williams* [1925] 1 KB 340.

96 Ibid.

97 *Crimes Act 1900* (NSW) s 61HA(5)(a); *Crimes Act 1958* (Vic) s 36(f); *Criminal Code* (Qld) s 348(2)(f); *Crimes Act* (SA) s 46(3)(g); *Criminal Code* (Tas) s 2A(2)(g); *Crimes Act 1900* (ACT) s 67(1)(f); *Criminal Code* (NT) s 192(2)(e).

98 *R v Pryor* [2001] QCA 24; See also *R v Gallienne* [1964] NSWR 919.

mistaken belief the accused was her partner. The burglar was convicted of rape. NSW further provides that there is no consent where the complainant mistakenly believes that he or she was married to the accused.[99]

Any type of fraud

WA, Tasmania, and the ACT notably recognise that consent can be invalid where obtained by any type of material fraudulent misrepresentation practised by the accused.[100] Commentators have long contemplated what these more expansive categories of fraud might look like.[101] The Court in *Michael v Western Australia* specifically considered that the WA legislation at least encompassed the types of fraud recognised in *Papadimitropoulos.*[102]

The case law on the relevance of fraud to questions of consent under Australian rape law has been fairly limited in scope, with legislative provisions concerning fraud and consent rarely being considered by appellate courts.[103] Another limitation that was outlined by Crowe (2014) was that each state and territory in Australia has significant interpretative difficulties regarding the exact content and boundaries of the categories of fraud.[104] Crowe (2014) maintains that the precise categories of fraud that can override consent have differed subtly between jurisdictions and also stipulates that the relevance of fraud for the purposes of Australian rape law has been largely neglected in the literature.[105] The limitations of the Australian legal system in relation to the circumstances where fraud can vitiate consent to sexual intercourse are explored further by Crowe (2014), who describes the methods in which the states and territories have handled the issues of fraud and consent as an approach affiliated with 'vagueness' and 'serious problems'.[106]

Another issue regarding fraud and rape and how consent is viewed lies in the finding that whilst all of the states and territories in Australia

99 *Crimes Act 1900* (NSW) s 61HA(5)(b).

100 *Criminal Code* (WA) s 319(2)(a); *Criminal Code* (Tas) s 2A(f); *Crimes Act 1900* (ACT) s 67(1)(g).

101 Crowe (n 89) 236; George Syrota, 'Rape: When Does Fraud Vitiate Consent?' (1995) 25 *Western Australian Law Review* 25; Jonathan Crowe, 'Consent, Power and Mistake of Fact in Queensland Rape Law' (2011) 23(1) *Bond Law Review* 21; Amit Pundik, 'Coercion and Deception in Sexual Relations' (2015) 28 *Canadian Journal of Law and Jurisprudence* 9.

102 *Michael v Western Australia* [2008] WASCA 66.

103 Crowe (n 89) 236, 236.

104 Ibid.

105 Ibid.

106 Crowe (n 89) 236, 237.

provide lists of circumstances in which consent is deemed not to be freely given for legal purposes,[107] not all jurisdictions have amended their lists so as to give consideration to the more recent and somewhat uncommon types of fraud which can occur in rape and sexual assault situations. Also, not all of the jurisdictions maintain a consistent view of the reasoning in *Papadimitropoulos*, with an example being that s 46(3) of the *Criminal Law Consolidation Act 1935* (SA) provides that a person does not freely and voluntarily consent to sexual intercourse if:

> (e) the person agrees to engage in the activity with a person under a mistaken belief as to the identity of that person; or
> (f) the person is mistaken about the nature of the activity.[108]

There are significant exceptions to this modelling which are evident in the WA, Tasmanian, and ACT provisions, which define the types of factors that can vitiate consent to sexual activity in a more generalised method.[109] Crowe (2014) thus explains that these jurisdictions treat any kind of deception which involves some kind of fraudulent misrepresentation as having the potential to legally vitiate consent to sexual intercourse.[110]

It can be gleaned from the analyses shown by Crowe (2014) that all of the Australian jurisdictions inevitably differ in the extent to which they recognise that consent to sexual intercourse has the potential to be vitiated by instances of fraud that go beyond the categories shown in *Papadimitropoulos*.[111]

Capacity

Most jurisdictions specify there is no consent where the complainant lacks the capacity to understand the sexual nature of the act.[112] Lack of capacity in sexual relations may relate to the complainant's age or impaired intellect. In *R v Howard*,[113] the applicant was convicted of

107 Ibid 238.
108 *Criminal Law Consolidation Act 1935* (SA) s 46(3).
109 *Criminal Code Act* (Tas) s 2A(2); *Criminal Code* (WA) s 319(2)(a); *Crimes Act 1900* (ACT) s 67.
110 Crowe (n 89) 236, 238.
111 Ibid.
112 *Crimes Act 1900* (NSW) s 61HA(4)(a); *Crimes Act 1958* (Vic) s 36(2)(g); *Crimes Act 1935* (SA) s 46(f); *Criminal Code* (Tas) s 2A(2)(i); *Crimes Act 1900* (ACT) s 67(1)(j); *Criminal Code* (NT) s 192(2)(d).
113 [1965] 3 All ER 984.

attempted rape of a six-year-old girl. The Court held that the issue of consent could not arise, as the child was incapable of consenting.[114]

The age of consent varies in each jurisdiction. In Victoria, a child under the age of 12 is incapable of consenting to participating in or viewing any sexual act.[115] Between the ages of 12 and 15, a person cannot consent to a sexual act with a person who is more than two years older than them. It is however not an offence if the person believed that the person was 16 years old, or if there is less than two years age difference between the parties.[116]

From the age of 16 years onwards a person has sexual autonomy/capacity to consent to sexual acts.[117] However, between the ages of 16 and 17 a person cannot consent to sexual acts with a person who is responsible for caring or supervising the individual. It is similarly not an offence if the person believed the individual was 18 years old or older.[118]

Case study: existing legal provisions relating to unprotected sex

The criminal law in Australia acknowledges the dangers associated with unprotected sex in certain occurrences. The criminal law statutes in each state and territory contain various sections which proscribe HIV transmission in certain situations. For instance, the law recognises the attraction of criminal liability where one partner puts the other partner at risk of the 'unwanted physical transformation of the profound life consequence of HIV through unprotected sex'.[119] Statutes either contain a precise offence relating to the transmission of diseases or provide assault-based offences where an HIV-infected individual has intentionally, recklessly, or negligently caused 'harm' to an individual by transmitting the disease.[120] The courts in Australia, and other jurisdictions, have subsequently imposed criminal liability where such transmission has occurred.[121] Certain judicial authority has relied on an assumption that the non-disclosure of HIV between two sexual partners vitiates otherwise valid consent. The Supreme Court of Canada held in *R v*

114 Ibid.

115 *Crimes Act* (Vic) s 49A.

116 *Crimes Act* (Vic) s 49B.

117 Ibid.

118 Ibid s 49E.

119 Leah A Plunkett 'Contraceptive Sabotage' (2014) 28(1) *Columbia Journal of Gender and Law* 97, 102.

120 *Crimes Act 1900* (NSW) s 33; *Criminal Code* (Qld) s 317; *Crimes Act 1935* (SA) s 7A; *Criminal Code* (WA) s 4(a); *Criminal Code* (NT) s 174B; *Crimes Act 1958* (Vic) s 18.

121 *R v Dica* [2004] EWCA Crim 1103; *R v Cuerrier* [1998] 2 S.C.R. 371; *R v Neil* (1909) 8 CLR 671; *Zaburoni v The Queen* (2016) 256 CLR 482.

Cuerrier that a failure to disclose one's HIV-positive status to a partner before sexual intercourse could amount to fraud vitiating consent to unprotected sexual intercourse, and that the sexual contact poses a significant risk of, or causes, serious bodily harm.[122] The Court conclusively viewed that it is not necessary that the complainant is infected with the virus; mere exposure is sufficient to attract criminal liability in these instances. The rationale is that had the complainant known that the respondent was HIV positive, they would never have engaged in unprotected intercourse with the offender.[123] McLachlin J stated that:

> Where the person represents that he or she is disease free, and consent is given on that basis, deception on that matter goes to the very act of assault. The complainant does not consent to the transmission of diseased fluids into his or her body. This deception in a very real sense goes to the nature of the sexual act, changing it from an act that has certain natural consequences (whether pleasure, pain or pregnancy) to a potential sentence of disease or death. It differs, [from other types of deception] in a profoundly serious way that merits the criminal sanction.[124]

This decision was later adopted in *R v Williams* where the Court held that there cannot be factual consent between sexual partners without the disclosure of HIV status.[125] Other common law countries have similarly adopted this 'aggressive'[126] approach. In *KSB v Accident Compensation Corp*,[127] the New Zealand Court of Appeal held that the non-disclosure of HIV-positive status prior to engaging in unprotected sexual intercourse does vitiate consent.

Fault element

The fault element of sexual offences focuses on the state of mind of the accused, or the *mens rea*, which must be established beyond reasonable doubt to determine liability.[128] The accused's state of mind will always

122 *R v Cuerrier* [1998] 2 SCR 371.
123 Ibid.
124 Ibid 412, 413.
125 *R v Williams* [1922] All ER 433.
126 *J KSB v Accident Compensation Corp* [2012] NZAR 578, Joanna Manning, 'Criminal Responsibility for the Non-disclosure of HIV-Positive States before Sexual Activity' (2013) 20(3) *Journal of Law and Medicine* 493, 496.
127 [2012] NZAR 578.
128 ALRC (n 2) 1158.

be a relevant factor irrespective of whether consent has been raised by the defence.[129] For example, if the prosecution is satisfied beyond reasonable doubt that the accused had sexual intercourse with the complainant, and that the complainant did not consent, the prosecution must then consider whether the accused knew that the complainant was not consenting.

The fault element for common law rape was established in the 1976 case of *DPP v Morgan* as an intention to have sexual intercourse without consent.[130] This intent will be satisfied by either knowledge that the victim is not consenting or recklessness as to whether the victim is consenting. The statutory formations in most jurisdictions reflect some variation of this formulation. In Queensland, WA, and Tasmania, the fault element for rape is an intention to have intercourse.[131] In NSW, ACT, and the NT, the fault element is an intention to have intercourse where the accused knows the complainant does not consent, or the accused is reckless as to whether the complainant is consenting.[132] However, in SA, the fault element is that the accused knows, or is recklessly indifferent to, the fact that the other person does not consent.[133] Victoria reformed its complex and widely criticised fault element in 2016 to a standard of whether a person 'reasonably believes' that another person has consented.[134] Victoria has additionally legislated jury directions around reasonable belief in consent, as discussed above.[135]

Recklessness

Recklessness is included in the statutory definition of rape in several jurisdictions. In SA, a person is recklessly indifferent to the fact that another person does not consent if they have failed to take reasonable steps to ascertain whether the person is consenting.[136] Further, the SA jurisdiction expressly incorporates an objective element to recklessness. That is, a person is also recklessly indifferent if they are aware, ought

129 *R v Olugboja* [1982] QB 320.
130 [1976] AC 182.
131 *Criminal Code* (Qld) s 349; *Criminal Code* (WA) s 325; *Criminal Code* (Tas) s 185.
132 *Crimes Act 1900* (NSW) s 61HA(3); *Crimes Act 1900* (ACT) s 54(1); *Criminal Code* (NT) s 192(4).
133 *Crimes Act 1935* (SA) s 46–47.
134 *Crimes Act 1958* (Vic) s 38(2)(a). See Simon Bronitt and Bernadette McSherry, *Principles of Criminal Law* (Thomson Reuters (Professional) Australia, 4th ed, 2017) 694.
135 *Jury Directions Act 2015* (Vic) s 47.
136 *Crimes Act 1935* (SA) s 48(1).

to have been aware, or did not give any thought to whether a person is consenting.

NSW is said to have the most comprehensive approach among jurisdictions.[137] While not defined in the NSW legislation, recklessness may be established where the accused: (1) realised the possibility that the complainant was not consenting but nevertheless continued or (2) failed to consider whether or not the complainant was consenting notwithstanding the risk that the complainant's lack of consent would have been obvious to someone with the accused's mental capacity if they considered it.[138] The criminalising of non-advertent recklessness reflects the common law decision of *R v Kitchener* where Kirby P considered that 'to excuse the reckless failure of the accused to give a moment's thought to [non-consent], is self-evidently unacceptable'.[139]

Defences

The accused's honest belief in consent is a full defence to rape in all jurisdictions. In SA and the ACT, this common law defence dictates that the honest belief in consent need not be reasonable.[140] The defence of honest, but unreasonable, belief was first considered in *DPP v Morgan*.[141] In that case, the complainant's husband invited the three co-accused men to have sexual intercourse with his wife and that any resistance from her was just a pretence. The men proceeded to forcibly have sexual intercourse with the complainant and were found guilty of rape. The men unsuccessfully appealed on the basis that they held an honest belief that the complainant was consenting. While the accused were not acquitted in this case, the House of Lords considered it was possible for an accused to be acquitted on the basis of an honest belief or mistake in consent.[142]

In all other jurisdictions, the belief in consent must be both honest and reasonable.[143] Proof that the accused's belief in consent was unreasonable will negate the defence of consent and prove the fault element of rape.

137 ALRC (n 2) 1160.
138 Criminal Justice Sexual Offences Taskforce, Attorney-General's Department (NSW), *Responding to Sexual Assault: The Way Forward* (2005) 43.
139 (1993) 29 NSWLR 696, 697 (Kirby P).
140 *DPP v Morgan* [1976] AC 182.
141 Ibid.
142 Ibid.
143 *Criminal Code* (Qld) s 348A; *Criminal Code* (WA) s 24; *Criminal Code* (NT) s 32; *Crimes Act 1958* (Vic) s 36A; *Crimes Act 1900* (NSW) s 61HA(3).

In Queensland, it is open for an accused to argue that they had an 'honest and reasonable, but mistaken belief' that the complainant was consenting.[144] Such an approach controversially shifts the focus to the question of what the defendant believed during the act and whether their mistake was honest and reasonable.[145] This has 'undesirable and socially regressive consequences', providing a 'back-door way' for factors such as the complainant's lack of overt resistance, level of intoxication, dress, prior behaviour and relationships to be presented as relevant factors.[146] For example, the case of *R v Dunrobin* illustrates the potential for passive compliance or 'freezing' by the complainant (even following initial resistance) to provide a basis for arguing this defence.[147] In this case, the complainant was asleep in the house of a friend of the accused when she awoke to the accused lying next to her. The accused asked the complainant for sexual intercourse and when she refused, he climbed on top of her and groped her breasts while she repeatedly told him to stop and physically pushed him off. He proceeded to undress the complainant and have intercourse with her. The complainant testified that whilst she continued to tell the accused to stop, she 'froze in a way' because she was scared. The Court of Appeal upheld the appeal on the basis that the jury has been improperly directed on the issue of mistake of fact.[148] Fryberg J specifically held that any 'expressions of negativity and physical resistance' should be mentioned by the trial judge when directing the jury on s 23.[149] The accused was ultimately considered to have a reasonable belief that the complainant was consenting, partially contributed by his paranoid schizophrenia, which was believed to be 'relevant to the appreciation of what, on his part, constituted a reasonable belief'.[150]

A more progressive model of this defence is believed to be adopted in the state of Tasmania. Section 14A(1) of the *Tasmanian Criminal Code*, as amended in 2004, reads as follows:

144 *Criminal Code* (Qld) s 348A.

145 Ibid.

146 Jonathan Crowe and Bri Lee, 'The Mistake of Fact Excuse in Queensland Rape Law' (2020) *University of Queensland Law Journal* 39(1) 1, 3.

147 *R v Dunrobin* [2013] QCA 175.

148 Ibid.

149 Ibid.

150 Ibid.

> In proceedings for [rape, indecent assault, or unlawful sexual intercourse], a mistaken belief by the accused as to the existence of consent is not honest or reasonable if the accused –
> (a) was in a state of self-induced intoxication and the mistake was not one which the accused would have made if not intoxicated; or
> (b) was reckless as to whether or not the complainant consented; or
> (c) did not take reasonable steps, in the circumstances known to him or her at the time of the offence, to ascertain that the complainant was consenting to the act.[151]

Based on this model, it is suggested that an accused is unable to rely on the defence of mistake of fact where they acted with disregard for the complainant's sexual autonomy.[152] This is because, pursuant to this model, a defendant cannot rely on mistakes caused by self-induced intoxication and section 14A also imposes responsibility for recklessness.[153] Moreover, the defendant is required to take reasonable steps to determine whether the complainant was consenting to the act.[154]

Jury directions

It is considered that the task of clarifying the laws of consent and establishing appropriate standards for sexual relations ought to be the role of a judge when explaining consent to a jury.[155] Jury directions are a set of instructions delivered by a judge to the jury at the conclusion of the trial. In their 2004 report, the Victorian Law Reform Commission (VLRC) recommended a number of legislative changes, including the amendment of jury directions to reflect the proposed communicative model of consent, and the simplification of existing directions to ease confusion.[156] In its submissions, the VLRC suggested that jury directions regarding consent were the most likely reform to alter legal approaches and outcomes in rape cases.[157]

151 *Criminal Code Act 1924* (Tas) s 14A(1).
152 Crowe (n 101) 21, 28.
153 Ibid.
154 Ibid.
155 Asher Flynn and Nicola Henry, 'Disputing Consent: The Role of Jury Directions in Victoria' (2012) *Current Issues in Criminal Justice* 24(2) 167, 168.
156 Victorian Law Reform Commission (VLRC), *Sex Offences: Interim Report*, Report No 78 (2004) Chapter 7.
157 Ibid.

Only two Australian jurisdictions, Victoria and the NT, have legislated jury directions about consent.[158] Jury directions aim to fulfil an educative function by 'clarifying the law and establishing standards of behaviour for sexual relations which are based on principles of communication and respect'.[159] These directions reinforce the communication model of consent and renounce stereotypical views of sexual roles.[160] Under these provisions, the judge must direct the jury on the meaning of consent and the circumstances under the legislation where consent is negated. Importantly, the jury must be directed that a person is not regarded as having consented merely because they did not protest, physically resist, or sustain an injury.[161] In Victoria, the judge must also direct the jury about the accused's awareness of the presence of consent in instances where the accused raises consent as a defence.[162] The jury must consider whether the belief in consent was reasonable, whether there is any evidence of that belief, and whether the accused took any steps to ascertain consent.[163]

In Victoria, the direction on consent is contained in section 46 of the *Jury Directions Act 2015* (Vic):[164]

Direction on consent

(1) The prosecution or defence counsel may request under section 12 that the trial judge direct the jury on consent.

(2) In making a request referred to in subsection (1), the prosecution or defence counsel (as the case requires) must specify –

  (a) in the case of a request for a direction on the meaning of consent – one or more of the directions set out in subsection (3); or

  (b) in the case of a request for a direction on the circumstances in which a person is taken not to have consented to an act – one or more of the directions set out in subsection (4).

158 *Jury Directions Act 2015* (Vic) s 46–7; *Criminal Code* (NT) s 192A.

159 Victorian Law Reform Commission (VLRC), *Sex Offences: Interim Report,* Report No 78 (2004) Chapter 7.

160 ALRC (n 2) 1170.

161 Ibid.

162 *Jury Directions Act 2015* (Vic) s 47.

163 Ibid.

164 *Jury Directions Act 2015* (Vic) s 46.

Note

Section 36 of the Crimes Act 1958 provides that consent means free agreement. That section also sets out circumstances in which a person has not consented to an act.

(3) For the purposes of subsection (2)(a), the prosecution or defence counsel may request that the trial judge –

(a) inform the jury that a person can consent to an act only if the person is capable of consenting and free to choose whether or not to engage in or allow the act; or

(b) inform the jury that where a person has given consent to an act, the person may withdraw that consent either before the act takes place or at any time while the act is taking place; or

(c) inform the jury that experience shows that –

(i) there are many different circumstances in which people do not consent to a sexual act; and

(ii) people who do not consent to a sexual act may not be physically injured or subjected to violence, or threatened with physical injury or violence; or

(d) inform the jury that experience shows that –

(i) people may react differently to a sexual act to which they did not consent and that there is no typical, proper or normal response; and

(ii) people who do not consent to a sexual act may not protest or physically resist the act; or

Example

The person may freeze and not do or say anything.

(e) inform the jury that experience shows that people who do not consent to a sexual act with a particular person on one occasion, may have on one or more other occasions engaged in or been involved in consensual sexual activity—

(i) with that person or another person; or

(ii) of the same kind or a different kind.

(4) For the purposes of subsection (2)(b), the prosecution or defence counsel may request that the trial judge—

(a) inform the jury of the relevant circumstances in which the law provides that a person does not consent to an act; or

(b) direct the jury that if the jury is satisfied beyond reasonable doubt that a circumstance referred to in section 36 of the **Crimes Act 1958** existed in relation to a person, the jury must find that the person did not consent to the act.

Whilst there has been extensive reform in Victoria concerning jury directions on rape cases, there remain several convoluted and somewhat complex jury directions on the functions of criminal law when dealing with rape charges.[165] The issues surrounding unclear jury directions and the subsequent problems concerning directions on how consent should be viewed in rape trials, has led to further confusion in this area of the law and has thus strayed away from the intended purpose of the reforms that have been enacted over the past two decades.[166]

Consent in the United Kingdom

Like the laws on sexual offending in many of its Western counterparts, the laws regarding consent in the United Kingdom have seen considerable change over time.

In early feudal England, the concept of consent was contemplated as early as 1285 in the amendments made to the second statute of Westminster.[167] The links between consent and rape were not made until the 1845 case *R v Camplin*[168] where the criminal element of 'against her will' was taken to mean 'non-consensual', as opposed to requiring force.[169]

Despite this legal clarity, subsequent judgements affirmed the antiquated requirements of rape (force and physical resistance), and this resulted in an 'incoherent' legal structure and deficiencies in law that persisted until the 1956 suite of legislative changes which paved the way for the current act.[170]

Like Australia, consent to sexual intercourse in the UK is governed by the common law and the relevant criminal law statute, namely the *Sex Offences Act 2003* (UK) (SOA).[171] The SOA was introduced in the early 2000s to replace archaic laws in respect of several sex offences and with an aim of improving rape convictions. The SOA came into effect on 1 May 2004 and applies to all offences committed on or after that date. The SOA repealed most of the previous legislation whilst also amending the sentencing guidelines and options.

165 Flynn and Henry (n 155) 167, 174.
166 Ibid.
167 James Stephen, *A History of the Criminal Law of England* (Macmillan, 1883), 202.
168 (1845) 1 CAR & K 746.
169 Omar Madhloon, 'Protecting Autonomy in Non-Consensual Sexual Offences: A Kantian Critique' (MPhil thesis, De Montfort University, 2014), 87.
170 Jack Vidler, 'Ostensible Consent and the Limits of Sexual Autonomy' (2017) 17 *Macquarie Law Journal* 103, 105.
171 *Sex Offences Act 2003* (UK).

Sections 1–4 of the *Sex Offences Act 2003* set out a range of offences which require the prosecution to prove an absence of consent. These offences are:

- Rape,
- Assault by penetration,
- Sexual assault, and
- Causing a person to engage in sexual activity.

In instances where it cannot be proved that the relevant offence occurred before or after 1 May 2004, the *Violent Crime Reduction Act 2006* applies instead.[172]

Definition of consent

Prior to 2003 there was no statutory definition consent. However, the current definition of consent is still referred to in cases pre-dating SOA to assist the jury's approach to determining any issue of consent.[173]

The SOA introduced a statutory definition of consent. Section 74 of the SOA defines consent as: 'a person consents if he agrees by choice and has the freedom and capacity to make that choice'.[174]

Section 79(2) of the SOA states that penetration is a continuing act from entry to withdrawal.[175] Accordingly, where an accused lacks the mens rea for rape at the initial penetration, they may commit an offence if at any stage they become aware of the complainant's lack of consent, and do not immediately withdraw.[176]

Intoxication and consent

A complainant is not considered to be consenting if the complainant is intoxicated by alcohol or affected by drugs.[177]

172 *Violent Crime Reduction Act 2006* (UK); Crown Prosecutors Service, *Rape and Sexual Offences* (Legal Guidance, 21 May 2021) Chapter 6.

173 Ibid.

174 *Sex Offences Act 2003* (UK) s 74.

175 *Sex Offences Act 2003* (UK) s 79(2).

176 *Kaitamaki v The Queen* [1985] AC 147; *Violent Crime Reduction Act 2006* (UK); Crown Prosecutors Service, *Rape and Sexual Offences* (Legal Guidance, 21 May 2021) Chapter 6.

177 *Violent Crime Reduction Act 2006* (UK); Crown Prosecutors Service, *Rape and Sexual Offences* (Legal Guidance, 21 May 2021) Chapter 6.

The Court in *R v Bree* [2007] EWCA Crim 804 considered:

> If, through drink (or for any other reason) the complainant has temporarily lost her capacity to choose whether to have intercourse on the relevant occasion, she is not consenting, and subject to questions about the defendant's state of mind, if intercourse takes place, this would be rape.
>
> However, where the complainant has voluntarily consumed even substantial quantities of alcohol, but nevertheless remains capable of choosing whether or not to have intercourse, and in drink agrees to do so, this would not be rape.[178]

Moreover, evidence that the complainant is unable to recollect the events that occurred cannot of itself be determinative of issues of consent and capacity.[179]

It is accepted that a complainant does not need to be unconscious to lose their capacity to consent and that an individual's capacity may diminish well before a complainant becomes unconscious.[180]

No requirement to prove consent

Many offences under the SOA do not require proof of an absence of consent. These circumstances are where the complainant is deemed incapable of consenting due to age or capacity.[181] These include:

- Rape of a child under 13
- Assault by penetration of a child under 13
- Sexual assault of a child under 13
- Inciting or causing a person to engage in sexual activity with a child under 13
- Child sexual offences involving children under 16
- Children under 18 having sexual relations with persons in a position of trust
- Children under 18 involved with family members over 18
- Persons with a mental disorder impeding choice

178 *R v Bree* [2007] EWCA Crim 804, [34].

179 *R v Bree* [2007] EWCA Crim 804, [34].

180 *R v Bree* [2007] EWCA Crim 804, [34].

181 *Violent Crime Reduction Act 2006* (UK); Crown Prosecutors Service, *Rape and Sexual Offences* (Legal Guidance, 21 May 2021) Chapter 6.

- Persons with a mental disorder who are induced, threatened, or deceived
- Persons with a mental disorder who have sexual relations with care workers[182]

Where there is an issue with respect of the complainant's capacity to consent to the act in cases of alleged rape, the consideration is left to the jury to determine.[183]

Evidential presumptions

Section 75 of the SOA provides a list of circumstances in which rebuttable evidential presumptions about the absence of consent apply.[184]

It is considered that, if the accused performed the relevant act (as defined in section 77), and the prosecution establishes that any of the circumstances specified in section 75(2) existed to the accused's knowledge, then the complainant is to be taken not to have consented and the accused is taken not to have a reasonable belief that the complainant was consenting.[185] In either case, the rebuttable presumption may be refuted by the accused with sufficient evidence to show the complainant did consent or that the accused did not have a reasonable belief in consent.

The applicable circumstances pursuant to section 75(2) are:

- Violence or fear of violence, subsection 2(a) and (b)
- Unlawful detention, subsection 2(c)
- Complainant asleep or unconscious, subsection 2(d)
- Complainant's physical disability, subsection 2(e)
- Administering a substance 2(f)

This evidence can derive from any source, such as from the cross-examination of a witness or from the defendant themselves.[186]

182 Ibid.
183 *R v Hysa* [2007] EWCA Crim 2056.
184 *Sex Offences Act 2003* (UK) s 75.
185 *Sex Offences Act 2003* (UK) s 75; *Violent Crime Reduction Act 2006* (UK); Crown Prosecutors Service, *Rape and Sexual Offences* (Legal Guidance, 21 May 2021) Chapter 6.
186 Ibid.

Conclusive presumptions

Section 76 of the SOA stipulates two conclusive presumptions where it is automatically presumed that the complainant did not consent to the act and where the accused did not reasonably believe that the complainant consented.[187]

These circumstances are where:

1 The accused intentionally deceived the complainant as to the nature or purpose of the relevant act; or
2 The accused intentionally induced the complainant to consent to the relevant act by impersonating a person known personally to the complainant.[188]

The first presumption was considered in the case of *R v Jheeta* [2007] EWCA Crim 1699. In this case the accused had repeatedly deceived the complainant to have sex with the accused on a more regular basis than she otherwise would have done, by a complicated and fabricated scheme.[189] The Court in this case considered that the complainant was not deceived as to the nature or purpose of the intercourse.[190] The Court therefore considered that the presumptions in section 76(2) had no application.[191]

Conditional consent

A series of prominent UK decisions have upheld that in addition to the circumstances outlined in section 76, there are other circumstances where ostensible consent is not valid consent.[192] This is where there is a material deception perpetrated on the complainant by the accused (other than those covered in section 76); or in circumstances where the accused failed to comply with a condition which the complainant imposed on the giving of his/her consent.[193]

187 *Sex Offences Act 2003* (UK) s 76.
188 Ibid.
189 *R v Jheeta* [2007] EWCA Crim 1699.
190 Ibid.
191 Ibid.
192 Crown Prosecutors Service, *Rape and Sexual Offences* (Legal Guidance, 21 May 2021) Chapter 6.
193 Ibid.

The case in *The Queen (on the app of F) v DPP*[194] concerned an example of 'conditional consent', being that the complainant had consented to intercourse on the basis that the accused would not ejaculate inside the vagina during intercourse. By the accused unilaterally deciding not to withdraw, the Court considered that the complainant was deprived of choice relating to the crucial feature on which her original consent to sexual intercourse was based. It was considered that the accused 'knowing that [the complainant] would not have consented, and did not consent to penetration or the continuation of penetration if she had any inkling of his intention, [...] deliberately ejaculated within her vagina'[195] and that this combination of circumstances fell within the statutory definition of rape.

The case of *R v Justine McNally*[196] did not involve a breach of conditional consent but was instead a deception as to a material fact of the act. This case involved a woman who deceived the complainant during intercourse that she was in fact a man. The Court considered that the victim chose to have a sexual encounter with a boy and her preference (her freedom to choose whether or not to have a sexual encounter with a girl) was removed by the accused's decision.[197] Accordingly, it was held that deception as to gender can vitiate consent.

Commentary around the case of *McNally* calls for caution in respect of deception as to gender,[198] specifically, recognising deception as to gender as the potential to disproportionately and unfairly impact the human rights of suspects who are transgender, where a requirement for communication around gender identification could cause detriment to those who do not identify under the traditional categories of sex and gender.[199] In attempt to avoid this outcome, prosecutors are bound by the duties set out in the *Equality Act 2010*; however, it is yet to be seen whether these obligations are adequate to mitigate the potential for discrimination under the criminal law.[200]

194 [2013] EWHC 945 (Admin).

195 Ibid.

196 [2013] EWCA Crim 1051.

197 Ibid.

198 *Violent Crime Reduction Act 2006* (UK); Crown Prosecutors Service, *Rape and Sexual Offences* (Legal Guidance, 21 May 2021) Chapter 6.

199 Claire Hogg, 'Review of Alex Sharpe's Sexual Intimacy and Gender Identity "Fraud": Reframing the Legal and Ethical Debate' (2021) 15(2) *Criminal Law and Philosophy* 323, 324.

200 Ibid.

These cases demonstrate that conditional consent is important to realising an indivudual's sexual autonomy.

The Court of Appeal in *R v Lawrance (Jason)*[201] clarified the circumstances that are capable of vitiating ostensible consent in respect of sex offences. The Court of Appeal considered that ostensible consent can be vitiated by deceptions that are closely connected to the nature or purpose of sexual intercourse. That is, the deception must relate to the physical performance of the sexual act rather than the wide-ranging circumstances surrounding it. Moreover, the communication of the deception is irrelevant.[202] The Court of Appeal clarified that it does not matter whether the suspect deliberately withholds information or states an explicit untruth – the fundamental issue will be whether the deception is sufficiently connected to the performance of the sexual act.[203]

Defences

Reasonable belief in consent

A consideration of whether a belief in consent is reasonable is determined with regard to all the circumstances, including any steps that the accused took to ascertain whether the complainant consented to the act.[204]

The *Sex Offences Act 2003* abolished the Morgan defence of a genuine, though unreasonably 'mistaken' belief as to the consent of the complainant.[205]

The accused has an overarching responsibility to ensure that the victim consents to the sexual activity at the time of the act. This test is a subjective test with an objective element. It will thereforc involve a consideration of whether:

1 The accused genuinely believed that the complainant consented (subjective element); and

201 [2020] EWCA Crim 971.

202 See, e.g., *R v B* [2006] EWCA Crim 2945, the Court of Appeal held the defendant's failure to disclose his HIV+ status did not vitiate consent. Moreover, the Court of Appeal in *R v McNally*, concluded that *R v B* left open whether an explicit lie might be capable of vitiating consent.

203 *R v Lawrance (Jason) [2020] EWCA Crim 971.*

204 *Sex Offences Act 2003* (UK) s 1(2).

205 Ibid; Crown Prosecutors Service, *Rape and Sexual Offences* (Legal Guidance, 21 May 2021) Chapter 6; *DPP v Morgan* [1976] AC.

2 If so, did the accused reasonably hold this belief (objective element).[206]

The objective element will be determined by a jury.

In determining whether the complainant was consenting, the Court of Appeal determined that there is no requirement that the complainant demonstrate or communicate a lack of consent to the accused.[207]

Consent in the United States

Rape is criminalised throughout the United States; however, the laws governing consent to sexual intercourse vary from state to state. Several case studies will be chosen amongst the states by way of comparison.

California

Section 261 of the *Cal Penal Code* ('PC') defines 'rape' as an act of sexual intercourse accomplished with a person, not the spouse of the perpetrator and without the consent of the person.[208] The offence of rape therefore requires two conditions to be met, being (1) that the act was against the victim's will and (2) that the victim was unable to consent.[209]

California rape law does not define 'sexual intercourse'. Instead, the PC construes what kind of acts constitute rape, being: all forms of non-consensual sexual assault may be considered rape, and any sexual penetration, however slight, is sufficient to complete the crime.[210]

The PC also contains express offences of sodomy, oral copulation, sexual battery, and unlawful sexual acts procured by fraud or false pretences.[211]

Against the victim's will

Section 261 of the PC specifies various circumstances where sexual intercourse will be considered to be against the victim's will.[212]

206 *Sex Offences Act 2003* (UK) s 1(c);(2).
207 *R v Malone* [1998] 2 Cr App R 447.
208 *Cal Penal Code* § 261.
209 Ibid.
210 *Cal Penal Code* § 263.
211 See, e.g., *Cal Penal Code* § 243, 289, 287.
212 *Cal Penal Code* § 261.

Rape is considered against a victim's will when the accused accomplished intercourse by way of one of the following elements:

- Force
- Violence
- Duress
- Fear of immediate bodily injury (to the victim or someone else)
- Threats of future retaliation against the victim (or another person), and there is a reasonable possibility that the accused will retaliate. 'Threaten to retaliate' in this context is taken to mean threats to kidnap, falsely imprison, or to inflict extreme pain, serious bodily injury, or death.
- Threats to use the authority of a public office to incarcerate, arrest, or deport someone.[213]

Capacity

If there is no evidence that intercourse was accomplished by force, threats, coercion, or fraud, it can also be proven that rape occurred by demonstrating that the victim did not consent or was unable to consent.[214]

A person will be deemed incapable of providing consent if they are unable to consent due to mental or physical incapacity that the accused was aware of, and if he or she was asleep or unconscious of the nature of the act and it is known to the accused.[215]

Unconscious of the nature of the act means that the victim was incapable of resisting because the victim was:

- Unconscious or asleep;[216]
- Was not aware, knowing, perceiving, or cognisant that the act occurred;[217]
- Was not aware, knowing, perceiving, or cognisant of the essential characteristics of the act due to the perpetrator's fraud in fact;[218] or
- Was not aware, knowing, perceiving, or cognisant of the essential characteristics of the act due to the perpetrator's fraudulent

213 Ibid.
214 Ibid.
215 See also *People v. Vukodinovich*, 238 Cal.App.4th 166, 189 (Cal. Ct. App. 2015).
216 *Cal Penal Code* § 261(a)(4)(A).
217 Ibid § 261(a)(3).
218 Ibid § 261.6.

representation that the sexual penetration served a professional purpose when it served no professional purpose.[219]

An accused will also be guilty of rape where the victim is prevented from resisting by any intoxicating or aesthetic substance or any controlled substance, and this condition was known or reasonably should have been known, by the accused.[220]

A person can only consent to sexual intercourse if they act freely and if they know the nature of the act. A person who consents to an act of intercourse may change his or her mind during the act. If the victim does so, the act of intercourse becomes non-consensual if:

- The victim communicated to the defendant that he or she objected to the act of intercourse and attempted to stop the act;
- The victim communicated the objection through words or acts that a reasonable person would have understood as showing a lack of consent; and
- The defendant forcibly continued the act of intercourse despite any objection.[221]

Non-spousal rape

While rape under section 261 of the PC requires the accused not to be married to the victim, it is still illegal to rape a spouse under section 262 of the PC, which carries the same elements and penalties as non-spousal rape.[222]

Notably, both sections define rape in terms of the inability of the victim to 'resist'. Such language is consistent with the common law understanding of rape as requiring physical or verbal resistance rather than positive consent.

Definition of consent

The model of consent under the PC requires consent to be freely given, reflecting a positive model of consent or 'affirmative consent'.[223]

219 Ibid § 261(a)(4)(A).
220 Ibid § 261(a)(3).
221 Ibid § 261(a).
222 Ibid § 262.
223 Ibid § 261.6.

In sections under the PC where consent is an issue (including sections 261 and 262 of the PC), 'consent' is defined pursuant to section 261.6 to mean positive cooperation in act or attitude pursuant to an exercise of free will.[224] To consent, the person must act freely and voluntarily and have knowledge of the nature of the act or transaction involved.[225] Consent cannot be procured by inducing fear in the victim.[226]

Section 261.6 also specifically states that a current or previous dating or marital relationship is not sufficient to constitute consent.[227]

Sentencing

Section 264.1 states the rape (as defined in sections 261 or 262), is punishable by imprisonment for a duration of three, six, or eight years.[228] A judge may also impose various fines if he or she sees fit.[229] For instance, where rape occurs between spouses, the court may order that the accused make payments to a battered womens' shelter for an amount up to a maximum of 1,000 dollars.[230]

Defence

Consent is a defence to rape under sections 261 and 262 of the PC; however, evidence that a victim asked the accused to use a condom (or other forms of birth control) is generally not a sufficient form of consent.[231]

224 Ibid § 261.6.
225 Ibid § 261.6.
226 See West's *Ann. Cal. Penal Code* § 266c 'Every person who induces any other person to engage in sexual intercourse, sexual penetration, oral copulation, or sodomy when his or her consent is procured by false or fraudulent representation or pretence that is made with the intent to create fear, and which does induce fear, and that would cause a reasonable person in like circumstances to act contrary to the person's free will, and does cause the victim to so act, is punishable by imprisonment in a county jail for not more than one year or in the state prison for two, three, or four years. As in the California Penal Code, "fear" means the fear of physical injury or death to the person or to any relative of the person or member of the person's family'.
227 *Cal Penal Code* § 261.6.
228 Ibid § 264.1.
229 *Cal Penal Code* § 264.1.

> in addition to any punishment imposed under this section the judge may assess a fine not to exceed $70.00 against any person who violates Section 261 or 262. The proceeds of the fine are to be used in accordance with Section 1463.23.

230 *Cal Penal Code* § 262.
231 See West's *Ann. Cal. Penal Code* § 261.7.

Alabama

The crime of rape in the first degree under the *Ala Criminal Code* (the Code) is defined as sexual intercourse where:

- The offender uses forcible compulsion against a member of the opposite sex; or
- The victim is incapable of consent by reason of being incapacitated; or
- The offender is 16 years of age or older and the victim is younger than 12 years old.[232]

Rape in the second degree occurs where the accused is 16 years or older and engages in sexual intercourse with a member of the opposite sex, and the victim is at least two years younger than the offender.[233] Second-degree rape also includes sexual intercourse with a victim who is 'mentally defective' under Alabama law.[234]

Sexual intercourse under the Code adopts an ordinary meaning of a male sexual organ penetrating a female sexual organ (ejaculation is not required).[235] This definition excludes rape perpetrated by women and same sex instances of rape.

The state of Alabama also contains an offence 'Sexual Torture', which prohibits penetration of the vagina, anus, or mouth of another person with an inanimate object by forcible compulsion, with the intent to sexually torture, sexually abuse, or to gratify the sexual desire of either party.[236] This offence also precludes incidences of physical injury, including burning, crushing, wounding, mutilating, or assaulting the sex organs or intimate parts of another person with the intent to sexually torture, abuse, or to gratify the sexual desire of either party.[237]

The Code also includes an offence of first- and second-degree sodomy that can be perpetrated only by a male.[238]

232 *Ala Code* § 13A-6-61.
233 Ibid § 13A-6-62.
234 Ibid.
235 Ibid § 13A-6-60.
236 Ibid § 13A-6-65.1.
237 Ibid.
238 Ibid § 13A-6-63; 13A-6-64.

Definition of consent

In Alabama, consent has been interpreted to mean 'acquiescence or compliance [with the proposition of another]'.[239] Lack of consent stems from either forcible compulsion or from being incapable of consenting.[240]

Forcible compulsion is defined as use or threatened use, whether express of implied, of physical force, violence, confinement, restraint, physical injury, or death to the threatened person or to another person.[241] Certain characteristics of the victim and accused are relevant in determining an implied threat which include, age, size, and any relevant mental or physical conditions.[242] It is also relevant to consider the extent to which the accused may have been in a position of authority, domination, or custodial control over the victim and also the atmosphere and physical setting in which the incident is said to have taken place.[243] Forcible compulsion is conclusive presumptive evidence of lack of consent.[244]

Consent in Alabama therefore does not require positive consent, or consent 'freely given'. Instead, a person is deemed not to consent in the circumstances above. Accordingly, this model of consent does not promote an affirmative model of consent, but instead only recognises the victim is not consenting in certain circumstances.

Capacity

According to the Code, a person is deemed incapable of consenting if he or she is incapacitated.[245] Incapacitated means that a person suffers from a mental or developmental disease or disability which renders the person incapable of appraising the nature of his or her conduct.[246]

A person is also deemed incapacitated if they are unable to give consent or unable to communicate an unwillingness to an act because the person is unconscious, asleep, or is otherwise physically limited or unable to communicate.[247]

239 *Ex Parte Gordon,* 706 So. 2d 1160, 1163 (Ala. 1997).
240 *Ala Code* § 13A-6-70(b).
241 Ibid § 13A-6-60.
242 Ibid § 13A-6-70.
243 Ibid § 13A-6-60(1).
244 *Ex Parte Gordon*, 706 So.2d 1160 (Ala. 1997).
245 *Ala Code* § 13A-6-70(c).
246 Ibid § 13A-6-60(2)(a).
247 Ibid § 13A-6-60(2)(c).

Moreover, incapacitation extends to where a person is temporarily incapable of appraising or controlling his or her conduct due to the influence of a narcotic, anaesthetic, or intoxicating substance, and the condition was known or should have reasonably been known to the offender.[248]

Defence

As it is an element to the offence of rape that the victim consents to the act, it flows that consent can form a defence to accusations of rape.[249]

An accused may use consent as a defence to accusations of rape even where the consent was 'implied', that is, where the consent was not expressed by the victim, but the conduct of the victim is such 'as to create in the mind of the accused an honest and reasonable belief that the victim consented to the act'.[250]

Voluntary intoxication by the accused can be a defence to the offence of rape, only if it amounts to 'insanity' and is 'of such a character and extent as to render [the accused] incapable of consciousness that he is committing a crime'.[251]

Sentencing

Rape in the first degree in Alabama is a Class A felony which attracts penalties of both imprisonment and the imposition of fines.[252] An offender can be imprisoned for life or not more than 99 years or less than 10 years.[253]

Rape in the second degree is a Class B felony which is also punishable by imprisonment and the imposition of financial penalties.[254] An offender shall be imprisoned for not more than 20 years, but not less than 2 years.[255]

248 Ibid § 13A-6-60(2)(b).
249 Ibid § 13A-6-70.
250 *Quirk v State*, 84 Ala. 435 (1888); *Allen v State*, 87 Ala. 107 (1889); *Taylor v State*, 249 Ala. 130 (1947).
251 *Wesson v State*, 644 So.2d 1302, 1313 (Ala. Crim. App. 1994).
252 *Ala Code* § 13A-6-61.
253 Ibid § 13A-5-6.
254 Ibid § 13A-6-62.
255 Ibid § 13A-5-6.

Conclusion

The definition of consent varies considerably from jurisdiction to jurisdiction in its scope and application. While there is no uniformity in definition, there are several key themes that can be taken from the various international definitions of consent:

1. Consent should be explicitly conveyed and offered freely.
2. Conditions of the sexual act should not be altered (e.g. removing condom) as this would require fresh consent.
3. Legislation is clearer where circumstances in which an individual is not consenting are outlined in the legislative provisions.

3 Stealthing

Stealthing[1]

Sexual violence is known to have debilitating effects on a complainant's self-esteem, confidence, and autonomy.[2] In 2017, Alexandra Brodsky published in the *Columbia Journal of Gender and Law* an article which addressed the obscure form of sexual violation known as `stealthing', or non-consensual condom removal.[3] Stealthing occurs when an individual removes a condom during sexual intercourse without the other person's knowledge or consent.[4] In a stealthing scenario, an individual has consented to 'protected' sex and typically only becomes aware of the condom's removal after intercourse has ended.[5] Whilst not a novel concept, media coverage in recent years has revealed the widespread occurrence of stealthing internationally.[6] In Australia, one in three women and one in five men who took part in a study conducted by Monash University in 2018 said they had been stealthed.[7]

1 This chapter draws heavily on the previously published work: Brianna Chesser and April Zahra, 'Stealthing: A Criminal Offence?' (2019) 31(2) *Current Issues in Criminal Justice* 217.

2 Criminal Justice Sexual Offences Taskforce, Attorney-General's Department (NSW), *Responding to Sexual Assault: The Way Forward* (2005) 10; Chesser and Zahra (n 1) 217.

3 Alexandra Brodsky, '"Rape-Adjacent": Imagining Legal Responses to Non-consensual Condom Removal' (2017) 32(2) *Columbia Journal of Gender and Law* 183.

4 Chesser and Zahra (n 1) 217.

5 Ibid.

6 Ibid.

7 Anne Crawford, 'Study Suggests "Stealthing" – Non-Consensual Condom Removal – A Common Practice', *Monash University* (Web Page 7 March 2019) www.monash.edu/medicine/news/latest/2019-articles/study-suggests-stealthing-non-consensual-condom-removal-a-common-practice.

DOI: 10.4324/9781003165606-3

The occurrence of stealthing is not exclusive to heterosexual intercourse, and while the majority of complainant accounts indicate that this crime is perpetrated by men, it is also possible for a female to 'stealth' her partner and remove the condom without her partner's consent, although such a scenario is reportedly less common.[8] Accordingly, both men and women can both be victims and perpetrators of stealthing.[9] The Monash University study found that most women who had been stealthed met the perpetrators through friends (29%) or sex work (23%).[10] In contrast, male victims of stealthing usually met their partners (also mostly male) through dating apps online.[11]

Stealthing presents a plethora of direct adverse consequences for complainants, including the risk of unintended pregnancy and the transmission of sexually transmitted infections (STIs).[12] Complainants also often experience severe psychological trauma, alongside feelings of guilt and shame associated with the violation of dignity and autonomy.[13] These negative feelings are reinforced by the ambiguity regarding the legality of what has occurred.[14]

Pop culture has recently depicted the prevalence of non-consensual condom removal in the HBO series *I May Destroy You*.[15] The series tells the story of a 36-year-old stealthing victim, Mia. Mia realised that she could no longer feel the condom after changing positions during intercourse. Mia asked her date where the condom was, and he 'shrugged'. As a result of the stealthing offence, Mia remembers feeling extremely confused and violated, which is a common occurrence among victims.

Perpetrators of stealthing are said to view their victims as a possession rather than individuals with the capacity to make their own consensual decisions about sex. Online communities exist that are dedicated to teaching men how to secretly remove a condom during sex and praising those who do so successfully.[16] Reasons cited by perpetrators on these online forums include that it 'feels better without a condom', for the

8 Chesser and Zahra (n 1) 217, 218.
9 Ibid.
10 Crawford (n 7).
11 Ibid.
12 Chesser and Zahra (n 1) 217, 218.
13 Ibid.
14 Ibid.
15 Kellie Scott, 'Stealthing in "I May Destroy You" Can Happen to Anyone. Here's What You Should Know', *ABC Everyday* (Web Page, 14 September 2020) www.abc.net.au/everyday/why-stealthing-is-a-violation-of-consent/12639172.
16 Ibid.

'thrill of degradation', and the exercise of a man's right to 'spread his seed'.[17]

Despite its prevalence, stealthing largely remains unreported. Only 1% of the respondents in the Monash University Study who had been stealthed reported the incident to the police.[18] The low incidences of reporting are partly attributable to the legal ambiguity surrounding the legality of stealthing. Where categories of sexual violence are not recognised by our legal system, and where a victim's account deviates from the stereotypical incidence of sexual assault, victims often blame themselves for the assault.[19] Accordingly, it is imperative that consent laws are inclusive and clear on modern sex crimes such as stealthing to aid victims in their recovery, and to ensure perpetrators are held accountable.[20]

Laws of consent

The criminalisation of sexual offences functions to prosecute those who have knowingly touched or penetrated the complainant in a way that they have not agreed to, thereby violating their sexual autonomy.[21] Assuming that the complainant is capable of consenting, consent to sexual intercourse is the factor that distinguishes legal from illegal sexual interaction.[22] Therefore, to attract criminal liability, non-consensual condom removal must be found to negate consent to sexual intercourse.

Stealthing and consent?

As discussed in Chapters 1 and 2, consent to sexual intercourse is most commonly based on the free agreement between sexual partners. This requirement is considered to uphold the sexual autonomy of an individual and protects their freedom to decide whether or not to engage in sexual intercourse.[23] Consent must be 'freely and voluntarily given' to

17 Ibid.

18 Crawford (n 7).

19 Chesser and Zahra (n 1) 217, 219; Criminal Justice Sexual Offences Taskforce (n 2) 9.

20 Chesser and Zahra (n 1) 217, 219.

21 *Criminal Law Review* (2015), Department of Justice and Regulation (Vic), Victoria's New Sexual Offence Laws 6. https://files.justice.vic.gov.au/2021-06/copy%20of%20cd%2015%20260259%20discussion%20paper%20victoria%20s%20new%20sexual%20offence%20laws%20an%20introduction%20web%20site%20version%203%20pdf.pdf.

22 Bianca Fileborn, Australian Institute of Family Studies, *Sexual Assault Laws in Australia* (ACSSA Resource Sheets) (2011) 7.

23 Australian Law Reform Commission (ALRC), *Family Violence – A National Legal Response,* Report No 114 (2010) 1150.

the conditions and circumstances of the particular act.[24] Accordingly, consent goes beyond mere acquiescence; it is characterised by an active willingness to participate in sexual activity, with no presence of coercion, force, or intimidation of any kind.[25] According to Brodsky (2017), stealthing can be considered to vitiate consent in two ways: under a literal approach and by a risks inherent approach.[26] A combination of both rationales provides a constructive description of how consent is vitiated in a stealthing scenario.

Literal approach

Stealthing vitiates consent, as it modifies the act an individual has initially consented to without acquiring fresh consent. The removal of the condom changes the 'literal' conditions of intercourse that consent was provided for, being the touch of a condom and not the touch of the skin of a penis.[27] The accused is consequently touching the complainant in a way that consent was not initially established upon, thereby violating their consent. Under these new circumstances, the accused would require fresh and informed consent for sex to continue on a consensual basis under the new conditions.[28] The complainant's initial consent is thus vitiated through the deliberate removal of the condom without their knowledge or agreement and the subsequent continuation of intercourse without fresh consent.

Risks inherent

Consent is further vitiated in a stealthing scenario on the basis that the consequences of the act are altered. The risks inherent rationale assumes the individual consents to a sexual act after contemplating the 'benefits and risks' of that behaviour.[29] A complainant of stealthing has consented to sexual intercourse on the understanding that they are engaging in condom-protected sex. It follows that, if the complainant had known that intercourse would be unprotected, they may not have initially granted consent to the act.[30] Such an assumption is realistic in

24 Ibid.
25 Ibid.
26 Brodsky (n 3) 183.
27 Ibid.
28 Ibid.
29 Ibid.
30 Shane M. Trawick, 'Birth Control Sabotage as Domestic Violence: A Legal Response' (2012) 100(3) *California Law Review* 721.

light of the adverse consequences that could ensue from unprotected sex, including unwanted pregnancy or the transmission of STIs.[31] Condom removal transforms the act into sexual intercourse where these risks are inherent and persuasively influence an individual's decision to engage in intercourse. Thus, consent to protected intercourse is not interchangeable with consent to unprotected intercourse. Stealthing vitiates consent, as it alters the conditions and consequences of the act an individual has consented to. Indeed, the courts have considered that if a complainant provides consent on the basis that the accused would use a condom, there would be no consent at all if the accused subsequently removed it.[32] In these circumstances it has also been contemplated that the consent may have been obtained by 'fraud', which can attract criminal liability.[33]

Does stealthing vitiate consent under current Australian law?

In October 2021 the ACT Legislatively Assembly passed the first legislative reform expressly criminalising stealthing in the world. The *Crimes (Stealthing) Amendment Bill 2021* amends s 67 of the *Crimes Act* to explicitly state that consent is negated by an 'intentional fraudulent representation' about the use of a condom during sex.[34]

The courts in Victoria could also soon join the ACT in classifying stealthing as a criminal offence.[35] In 2018, a prominent surgeon was charged with raping his male sexual partner (a physician) after he removed his condom without permission whilst they were having sex. The two had gone out for dinner and returned to the doctor's home and had intercourse. Despite assuring the doctor he would use a condom, the surgeon allegedly removed the condom without consent. The doctor made a complaint to the police and the surgeon was charged with one count of rape and one count of sexual assault. At this point in time, it

31 Brodsky (n 3) 183.

32 *Assange v Swedish Prosecution Authority* [2011] EWHC (Admin) 2849.

33 Ibid.

34 Harry Frost, 'Bill to Criminalise Stealthing, Removing a Condom during Sex without Consent, to Be Considered in ACT', *ABC News* (Article, 22 April 2021) www.abc.net.au/news/2021-04-22/stealthing-bill-criminalise-condom-removal-sex-consent/100085704.

35 Brianna Chesser, 'Case in Victoria Could Set New Legal Precedent for Stealthing, or Removing Condom during Sex', *The Conversation* (Web Page, 16 August 2019) https://theconversation.com/case-in-victoria-could-set-new-legal-precedent-for-stealthing-or-removing-condom-during-sex-118343.

is unclear whether the accused will be convicted of rape; however, a trial is set to take place in the near future.[36]

Separate from the recent legislative amendments in the ACT, the legality of stealthing in other Australian jurisdictions is unclear. To attract criminal liability in Australia stealthing must satisfy the *mens rea* and *actus reus* elements as outlined in Chapter 2. The courts may find that stealthing vitiates the 'free and voluntary' model of consent, or that it is a class of fraud vitiating consent under the legislative provisions of some Western common law countries. However, the courts may alternatively find that stealthing does not vitiate 'free and voluntary' consent, as the individual has consented to the physical act of intercourse, and it is therefore unlikely to be classed as fraud. Whether stealthing is likely to be classed as rape under the current legislative provisions will ultimately depend on the approach taken by the courts in interpreting and applying restrictive legislation.[37]

Definition of consent

On a literal interpretation of 'free and voluntary' consent, courts have proposed that 'free and voluntary consent' should embody the 'free choice' of an individual with the cognitive capacity to give it.[38] An individual is considered to be acting 'freely and voluntarily' when one 'acts free from circumstances constraining one's action'[39] or where one consents without force to the physical act of sexual intercourse.[40] An individual is furthermore considered to be acting voluntarily when they are actively engaged.[41] In instances of stealthing, an individual has typically provided voluntary, express, or implied consent to the physical act of sexual intercourse and/or sexual touching that they are actively engaged in. Complainants may also fail to act 'freely and voluntarily' in giving consent for reasons of incapacity.[42] However, a

36 Ibid.

37 Chesser and Zahra (n 1) 217, 222.

38 *R v Winchester* [2011] QCA 374 at [79] (Muir JA).

39 *Tonkiss v Graham* [2002] NSWSC 891 at [78], [79] (Campbell J); *R v Winchester* [2011] QCA 374, [79] (Muir JA).

40 *Michael v Western Australia* [2008] WASCA 66.

41 Simon Bronitt and Bernadette McSherry, *Principles of Criminal Law* (Thomson Reuters (Professional) Australia, 4th ed, 2017) 694.

42 *Tonkiss v Graham* [2002] NSWSC 891 at [76].

stealthing complainant will not necessarily fit into existing categories of complainants who are considered incapable of consenting.[43]

It is unclear whether the courts would recognise stealthing as falling beyond the bounds of free and voluntary agreement under current criminal law statutes. The courts may find that consent obtained under the mistaken belief that a condom would be used was not given 'freely' and 'voluntarily'. Certainly, the Court in *Assange*[44] noted that any deception surrounding condom use removes any free agreement by the complainant.[45] This is consistent with other judicial commentary which considers that condom usage forms part of the sexual activity in question, and an individual's voluntary agreement to sexual intercourse includes 'where on her[his] body [s]he was touched and with what'.[46] An individual who consents to sexual intercourse with a condom does not freely or voluntarily agree to intercourse where the condom is removed, as this changes the conditions of the sexual contact.

On the other hand, the courts may consider that free and voluntary consent relates only to the sexual activity in question, making collateral conditions such as condom use potentially irrelevant to the presence of consent. In a stealthing scenario, the court may find that the complainant has freely, without constraint, provided consent to a specific act of intercourse and is not incapable of consenting. This reflects the underlying societal acceptance that the presence of violence or resistance is indicative of 'real rape'.[47] The model of jury directions adopted in some jurisdictions such as Victoria, Australia, may ultimately contribute to combatting these 'real rape' myths and aid in the conviction of cases akin to stealthing.[48] Even if consent is considered to be obtained at this stage, there are a range of circumstances which may negate consent that is freely and voluntarily given.

Circumstances where consent is vitiated

The legislative provisions in each jurisdiction provide a non-exhaustive list of distinct circumstances where consent is deemed to be vitiated.

43 See, e.g., *Crimes Act 1900* (NSW), s 61HE(5)(6); *Crimes Act 1958* (Vic), s 36((2)e); *Crimes Act 1935* (SA), s 46(f); *Criminal Code* (Tas), s 2A(2)(i); *Criminal Code* (NT), s 192(2)(d).

44 *Assange v Swedish Prosecution Authority* [2011] EWHC (Admin) 2849.

45 Ibid.

46 *R v Hutchinson* [2014] 1 SCR 346.

47 Bronitt and McSherry (n 40) 694.

48 *Jury Directions Act 2015* (Vic), ss 46–47.

Separate from the recent ACT reform which inserts a direct reference to representations condom use,[49] most of these categories are insufficient or inappropriate to cover instances of stealthing, as stealthing does not usually involve force, the threat of force, or non-physical threats.[50] The complainant is similarly unlikely to be unlawfully detained, asleep, unconscious, or so affected by alcohol or drugs as to be unable to initially consent to sexual intercourse.[51] Finally, the accused may not be in an abusive position of authority or trust over the complainant.[52] While the presence of any of these factors in a stealthing scenario would indisputably vitiate the complainant's consent, the vitiating factor would be something other than the occurrence of non-consensual condom removal. As a result, except for the legislation in the ACT, these provisions do not adequately account for the typical stealthing scenario where non-consensual condom removal occurs independently of other vitiating circumstances.

Statutory fraud applied to stealthing

The common law prescribes that only two forms of mistake or fraud can form the basis of non-consensual sex: mistake or fraud about the identity of a person's sexual partner, or mistake or fraud about the fundamental nature of the act.[53] The High Court has expressed that this second category is to be interpreted narrowly, only encompassing instances where the fraud or mistake relates to the character of the physical act that was done.[54] Stealthing does not involve any mistake as to the accused's identity (as the complainant, by virtue of their consent, is aware of who they are engaging in intercourse with). Nor does it involve any mistake or fraud as to the nature of the act recognised by the courts, namely fraud that the act is of a medical nature or for a hygienic purpose rather than sexual.[55] Indeed, the English Court held in the case of

49 *Crimes Act 1900 (ACT)*, s 67(1)(h).

50 *Crimes Act 1900* (NSW), s 61HE(5)(c); *Crimes Act 1958* (Vic), s 36(2)(a); *Criminal Code* (Qld), s 348(2)(a); *Criminal Code* (WA), s 319(2)(a); *Crimes Act 1935* (SA), s 46(3)(a)(i); *Criminal Code* (Tas), 2A (2)(b); s 67(1)(a)–(c); *Criminal Code* (NT), s 192 (2)(a)).

51 *Crimes Act 1900* (NSW), s 61HE(5)(b); *Crimes Act 1935* (SA), s 46(3)(c); *Crimes Act 1958* (Vic), s 36(2)(c)(d); *Criminal Code* (Tas), s 2A(h); *Criminal Code* (NT), s 192 (2)(c)).

52 (*Criminal Code* (Qld), s 348(2)(d); *Criminal Code* (Tas), s 2A(2)(e); *Crimes Act 1900* (NSW), s 61HE(8)(c)).

53 *Papadimitropoulos v The Queen* (1957) 98 CLR 249.

54 Ibid.

55 See, e.g., *R v Williams* [1923] 1 KB 340; *R v Flattery* (1877) 2 QBD 410.

Assange, under s 76 of the *Sexual Offences Act 2003*, the accused's conduct in removing the condom during intercourse was deceptive, but not deceptive as to 'the nature or quality of the act'.

Fraud beyond the common law

The legislative provisions in most states have codified this position in *Papadimitropoulos* and recognised that consent is vitiated by mistake or fraud in these two circumstances.[56] However, WA, Tasmania, and the ACT treat any kind of material fraudulent representation as having the potential to legally vitiate consent to intercourse.[57] Such broad conditions may encompass stealthing, where the complainant has consented to sex under the mistaken belief that the intercourse would be protected. It is thus possible that a court may find that stealthing is akin to rape in these jurisdictions. There has been discussion about the likely interpretation of these broad sections, and it has been suggested that the vague wording of these sections is likely to result in judicial hesitance in interpreting these sections broadly.[58] Jurists and commentators have expressed fears that a broad interpretation of these sections could result in the 'truly dramatic' ramification of many failed seductions being classified as rape, for example, where an individual professes their false love for their partner in an attempt to seduce them.[59] As a result, Steyley J took the opportunity in Michael at [89] to suggest that the legislation be narrowed by Parliament to avoid overcriminalisation, rather than deferring to judicial discretion. However, Steyley J stated that the possible ramifications of a broad interpretation were a 'slender basis' to read down the section under the *Criminal Code* (WA).[60] Heenan AJA also stated in Michael at [62] that this broad section should only extend to the nature and purpose of the sexual act, as espoused in *Papadimitropoulos*.

The finding of rape in a stealthing scenario therefore may differ depending on whether the courts favour a broad or narrow interpretation of these sections. A narrow interpretation of these sections

56 *Crimes Act 1900* (NSW), s 61HE(6); *Crimes Act 1958* (Vic), s 36(f)–(h); *Criminal Code 1899* (Qld), s 348(2)(f); *Crimes Act 1935* (SA), s 46(3)(g); *Criminal Code 1924* (Tas), s 2A(2)(g); *Criminal Code 1983* (NT), s 192(2)(e)).

57 *Criminal Code 1913* (WA), s 319(2)(a); *Criminal Code 1924* (Tas), s 2A(f); *Crimes Act 1900* (ACT), s 67(1)(g).

58 Jonathan Crowe, 'Fraud and Consent in Australian Rape Law' (2014) 38(4) *Criminal Law Journal* 236.

59 Neil Morgan, 'Oppression, Fraud and Consent in Sexual Offences' (1996) 26 *University of Western Australia Law Review* 223; *Michael v Western Australia* [2008] WASCA 66.

60 *Michael v Western Australia* [2008] WASCA 66.

encompasses a variation of the fraud recognised in *Papadimitropoulos.* The High Court in *Papadimitropoulo*s at [260] recognised that it is that the 'identity of the man and the character of the physical act that is done or proposed [...] to which the woman's consent is directed'. The Court also noted that 'once the consent is comprehending [...] the inducing causes cannot destroy its reality and leave the man guilty of rape'. The focus of the law in instances of fraud is thus placed on the complainant's state of mind rather than the deceptive conduct of the accused: 'If a woman consented to an act knowing it to be an act of sexual intercourse, no mistake as to the man's purpose deprives her consent of reality'.[61] According to Crowe (2014), *Papadimitropoulos* tells us that consent fraudulently obtained ultimately involves a consideration of whether the complainant knew that what they were doing was engaging in sexual intercourse with the accused, despite the presence of fraud.[62] In a stealthing scenario, the complainant is under no illusion that sexual intercourse is about to occur; therefore, it could be consequently irrelevant that the accused has deceived their sexual partner regarding the purported condom use, as the complainant knew they were consenting to sexual intercourse. This is consistent with the holding in *Papadimitropoulos* that 'once the consent is comprehending and actual, the inducing causes cannot destroy its reality and leave a man guilty of rape'. In line with these principles, Australian courts taking a narrow approach would likely hold, in circumstances of stealthing, that the complainant has consented to the act of penetration with the misrepresentation of protection being viewed as an 'inducing cause'.[63] This is reflected in recent case law where the courts have considered misrepresentations as only going to the 'motive' of whether intercourse will occur and so are 'indirectly relevant' to consent.[64] Under this narrow approach of fraud, stealthing is unlikely to be recognised as vitiating consent, as it does not involve fraud as to the identity of the person nor is there fraud as to the character of the physical act (namely, it does not involve fraud that the act is for medical or hygienic purposes).

Under the current common law model, which has been largely codified in statute, some 'controversial cases' will fall outside the scope of consent laws, 'particularly those cases where the defendant has put a partner at risk of contracting a serious disease through sexual contact'.[65]

61 *R v Mobilio* [1991] VR 339 at [344].
62 Crowe (n 56) 236.
63 *Papadimitropoulos v The Queen* (1957) 98 CLR 249 at [261].
64 *R v Winchester* [2011] QCA 374 at [116].
65 Morgan (n 57) 223.

However, it remains unclear whether stealthing would classify as fraud vitiating consent under the legislative provision in the states, for example in WA, where any type of fraud or mistake is capable of vitiating consent. It is possible that the courts may consider that consent under the mistaken belief that intercourse would be protected is vitiated in these circumstances. This will ultimately depend on whether the courts favour a narrow or broad interpretation of these sections. Even if the legislation was to recognise fraudulent statements about condom usage, the present law of fraudulent consent would not be expansive enough to incorporate all instances of stealthing. Express prior agreement or statements regarding condom usage are not uniform in all instances of stealthing; indeed, the accused may not have actually represented that they will use a condom or that they will refrain from removing it.

State of mind of the accused

If the courts found that the complainant in a stealthing scenario was not consenting due to any of the reasons outlined above, the fault element must also be proven beyond reasonable doubt. This is necessary even where the complainant's lack of consent to condom removal is proven beyond reasonable doubt. In most states, the relevant fault element is the accused's intention to have intercourse, and awareness or recklessness as to the complainant's lack of consent.[66] In cases of stealthing, there is evidently an intention to have intercourse, which would satisfy the fault element in these states and territories. However, it is unclear whether the accused would be found to be aware or reckless as to the complainant's non-consent to sexual intercourse in situations where a preference for condom use is not expressly communicated.

Interestingly, the recent ACT reform requires a person to make an 'intentional' misrepresentation about the use of a condom.[67] Accordingly, this offence only captures instances where the perpetrator's removal of the condom is accompanied by a positive statement about condom use. This may present challenges with proving that the perpetrator intended to deceive the complainant and/or intended to remove the condom.

66 See, e.g., *Criminal Code* (Qld), s 349; *Criminal Code* (WA), s 325; *Criminal Code* (Tas), s 13; *Crimes Act* (NSW), s 61HE(3); *Criminal Code* (NT), s 192 (4)b; *Crimes Act* (Vic), s 38(2)).

67 *Crimes Act 1900(ACT)*, s 67(1)(h).

Accused was aware

The prosecution may face difficulties proving this element in the absence of any form of communication of non-consent to sexual intercourse without a condom. While the substantive law no longer requires evidence of physical resistance or an outward manifestation of a lack of consent, empirical evidence reveals that convictions are difficult to obtain without evidence of resistance.[68] A complainant of stealthing will typically be unaware that intercourse is going to occur without a condom, and so is unlikely to indicate any signs of non-consent until after the intercourse has concluded. Furthermore, where there is no prior discussion or express agreement around condom usage, an accused may contend that they were not aware the complainant's consent was conditional on condom use.

Whether a judge would find this belief reasonable is uncertain given the court's often strict application of this standard. For example, in the case of *R v Lazarus*,[69] the parties accepted that the complainant had not consented to anal sex with the accused. However, it was found that the accused did have a genuine and honest belief that she consented, despite that 'in her own mind' she did not consent. The accused was ultimately acquitted of the crime, in part because it was unclear that the complainant took 'any physical action to move away'.[70] Following this case, the NSW fault element has received criticism for not being 'clear' or 'fair enough', prompting the NSW Attorney-General to refer the statute to the consideration of the Law Reform Commission.[71]

The present application of these provisions is often focused around the complainant's conduct, which means that the courts would likely find in a similar way in a stealthing scenario. The unaware complainant may not show any aversion, and therefore the accused may not be 'aware' that the complainant does not consent. In Victoria, the accused must 'reasonably believe' that another person is consenting to penetration.[72] In a stealthing scenario, the courts may find that an accused would reasonably be aware that the complainant may not consent to sex

68 Bree Cook, Fiona David, and Anna Grant, Attorney-General's Department (Cth), '*Sexual Violence in Australia*' (Research Paper No 36) Canberra: Australian Institute of Criminology).

69 *R v Lazarus* [2017] NSWCCA 279.

70 Ibid.

71 Louise Milligan and Lucy Carter, 'NSW Attorney-General Calls for Review of Sexual Consent Laws Following Four Corners Program', *ABC News* (Article, 8 May 2018) www.abc.net.au/news/2018-05-08/nsw-attorney-general-calls-for-review-of-sexual-consent-laws/9734988.

72 *Crimes Act 1958* (Vic), s 38(2)(b).

without a condom, given the risks that ensue from unprotected sex. The jury may further consider that the accused's failure to enquire whether the condom could be removed could count against the belief in consent being reasonable.[73]

Recklessness

In some jurisdictions there will be no consent where the accused may have realised the possibility that the complainant was not consenting but nevertheless continued.[74] This requires a consideration of whether the complainant was consenting and includes conduct which is 'negligent or careless' as well as that which is 'rash or incautious as to consequences'.[75]

Recklessness as to consent to condom removal may in some jurisdictions satisfy the fault element. The accused is plainly recklessly indifferent to the fact that the complainant is not consenting. Even without a prior discussion about the use of protection, with the increased risks associated with unprotected sex, the court may find it reasonable that the accused's intention to remove the condom without express permission could constitute reckless indifference to consent. In NSW, where this element encompasses both advertent and inadvertent conduct, it is highly likely that a person accused of stealthing would be held to have failed to consider whether the complainant was consenting, as the risk that the other person was not consenting would have been obvious to someone in the accused's position.[76] Some jurisdictions also consider recklessness as a failure to take reasonable steps to ascertain whether the complainant is consenting.[77] A failure to check whether the complainant consented to the condom removal is likely to be considered, at the very least, reckless and thus unreasonable. Importantly, the satisfaction of this fault element is inadequate on its own and must still be proven in conjunction with the complainant's lack of consent to attract liability.

73 *Criminal Law Review* (2015), Department of Justice and Regulation (Vic), Victoria's New Sexual Offence Laws 6.

74 See, e.g., *Crimes Act* (SA), s 48(1); *Crimes Act* (NSW), s 61HE(3); *R v Kitchener* (1993) 29 NSWLR 696.

75 *R v Kitchener* (1993) 29 NSWLR 696.

76 *Crimes Act* (NSW), s 61HE(3); *R v Kitchener* (1993) 29 NSWLR 696.

77 *Crimes Act* (SA), s 47.

Defence of honest and reasonable belief

In jurisdictions where the fault element is satisfied by a mere intention to have intercourse, the accused may raise the mistaken belief in consent as a defence to disprove the fault element. In some jurisdictions such as SA and the ACT, this defence is merely an honest belief that the individual was consenting.[78] This would be difficult to disprove in the absence of any form of communication of non-consent. In jurisdictions where this belief must be both honest and reasonable, or where the jury is directed as such, a defence of belief in consent may be more difficult to prove.[79] This defence is considered with reference to whether there were reasonable grounds for the accused to believe the complainant was consenting.[80] The outcome therefore turns on whether the jury finds the accused's belief reasonable. Given the risks that ensue from unprotected sex, such a belief in consent is likely to be considered unreasonable in a stealthing scenario, assuming that the jury is directed correctly.

Would the courts deem consent to be vitiated in Australia?

The legality of stealthing in the ACT has recently been clarified by legislative reform. However, an analysis of the substantive criminal law in the remaining states and territories in Australia reveals that it is unclear whether stealthing would be considered to vitiate consent. On one interpretation, the courts may find that an individual has not provided 'free and voluntary consent' in situations where they have consented under the mistaken believe that a condom is going to be used. However, another interpretation of the current model of 'free and voluntary' consent may find it inadequate to denounce the typical stealthing scenario where the complainant provides consent to the physical act of sexual intercourse (not consent to the removal of a condom). Furthermore, while stealthing does not fit into the traditional classes of fraud or mistake in most states, stealthing may satisfy the broader provisions of fraud in states such as WA. Again, this depends on the approach taken by the courts. Overall, if stealthing was found to satisfy the actus reus under these provisions, an accused would likely satisfy the fault element in some jurisdictions. The legality of stealthing largely depends on the approach the courts take in interpreting the current legislative provisions. In light of this ambiguity, legislative reform is required to

78 *Crimes Act* (SA), s 48(1); *Crimes Act* (ACT), s 54(1); *DPP v Morgan* [1976] AC 182.
79 *Criminal Code* (Qld), s 24; *Criminal Code* (WA), s 24; *Criminal Code* (NT), s 32; *Crimes Act* (Vic), s 36A; *Crimes Act* (NSW), s 61HE(3).
80 See also *R v Daniels* (1989) 1 WAR 435 at [445].

ensure that stealthing is appropriately classed as a sexual offence. Such reform has already been anticipated in a number of states and territories, as described below.

Does stealthing vitiate consent under current UK law?

Unlike most jurisdictions, stealthing has actually been the subject of judicial consideration in the United Kingdom.

In 2011, the UK High Court in *Assange* held that non-consensual condom removal could amount to liability for rape. In this case, the accused allegedly engaged in unprotected sex without the knowledge of the complainant, despite her prerequisite to sexual intercourse that a condom be used.[81] The High Court of Justice held at [87] that, pursuant to the definition of consent under the SOA, deception about protection could alone vitiate consent.[82] The complainant was considered not to be consenting because her consent carried the condition of condom use. The Court held at [86]:

> It would plainly be open to a jury to hold that, if the complainant had made clear that she would only consent to sexual intercourse if Mr Assange used a condom, then there would be no consent if, without her consent, he did not use a condom, or removed or tore the condom without her consent.[83]

The Court went on to state that if an accused has sexual intercourse in circumstances where the complainant has made it clear that they would only have sexual intercourse if the accused used a condom, the accused's conduct would amount to an offence under the SOA.[84]

The Court commented that the accused's conduct in having sexual intercourse with the complainant without a condom was deceptive as to the 'nature or quality of the act'.[85] However, as the provisions relating to deception under s 76 of the SOA are conclusive presumptions, the Court considered that the issue of the 'materiality' of condom use is to be properly determined pursuant to s 74 of the SOA (definition of consent).[86] It was ultimately considered that sexual intercourse without a condom is different to sexual intercourse with a condom, given the

81 *Assange v Swedish Prosecution Authority* [2011] EWHC (Admin).
82 Ibid [87].
83 Ibid [86].
84 Ibid.
85 Ibid [86]–[87].
86 Ibid.

presence of a physical barrier, a perceived difference in the degree of intimacy, the risks and potential for disease, and the prevention of pregnancy.[87]

The UK Courts later relied on the legal principles set out in Assange in the case of *R(F) v DPP & A*.[88] In this case, the Court found that a man who ejaculated inside his sexual partner despite earlier agreeing to refrain from doing so could face a conviction for rape. The accused and complainant were husband and wife and had previously agreed that the accused would use a condom or withdraw. On one occasion, the accused did not wear a condom, and refused to withdraw, later resulting in the complainant's pregnancy. The Court held that the deception about condom use, or the promise not to ejaculate, could be held to displace any free agreement by the complainant and so negated any consent. This was because the complainant 'was deprived of choice relating to the crucial feature on which her original consent to intercourse was based [and] accordingly her consent was negated'.[89]

In 2019, a Bournemouth man was convicted of removing a condom during intercourse with a sex worker who had made it clear prior to intercourse that wearing protection was a condition of her consent.[90] The rapist, Lee Hogben, was sentenced to 12 years' imprisonment.[91] This has been cited by legal professionals in the United Kingdom as an example of 'conditional consent'.[92] In recognising the developing prominence of this issue, the recently amended *Criminal Prosecution Service Guidance: Rape and Sexual Offence* contains detailed guidance on 'conditional consent'.[93] Such policy changes include that any cases of stealthing or those involving 'conditional consent' must be referred to the Principal Legal Advisor at the CPS in order to oversee the charging decision.[94]

87 Ibid.

88 *R(F) v DPP & A* [2014] QB 581.

89 Ibid [26].

90 Adam Forrest, 'Man Who Removed Condom during intercourse with Sex Worker Jailed for Rape', *Independent* (Web Page, 24 April 2019) www.independent.co.uk/news/uk/crime/rape-condom-sex-worker-unprotected-lee-hogben-guilty-bournemouth-a8884726.html.

91 Ibid.

92 Nick Dent, '"Stealthing" Conviction Brings Conditional Consent out in the Open', *Kingsley Napley* (Web Page, 3 May 2019) www.kingsleynapley.co.uk/insights/blogs/criminal-law-blog/stealthing-conviction-brings-conditional-consent-out-in-the-open#page=1.

93 *Violent Crime Reduction Act 2006* (UK); Crown Prosecutors Service, *Rape and Sexual Offences* (Legal Guidance, 21 May 2021) ch 6.

94 Ibid.

The 2020 Court of Appeal case in *R v Lawrance* gave further consideration to the circumstances in which deception is capable of vitiating consent to sexual intercourse.[95] The Court clarified in this case that ostensible consent can be vitiated by deception that is closely connected to the nature or purpose of the act.[96] The Court further determined that the manner of communication of the deception is irrelevant and that the fundamental issue is whether the deception was sufficient closely connected to the performance of the sexual act.[97]

Despite these judicial precedents, it is clear that not every case will amount to rape where a condom is not worn despite prior agreement to its use. Commentary indicates that prosecutors must still consider the overall context of the allegations and the extent to which the conduct is considered to negate the freedom of the complainant to determine their own sexual autonomy.[98]

Does stealthing vitiate consent under current US law?

Currently, no state in the United States explicitly deems that stealthing vitiates consent and the issue has not received any judicial attention before the courts.

The previous chapter provided a brief overview of the consent laws in California and Alabama. Unsurprisingly, under the laws in the state of Alabama, it is not likely that stealthing would be deemed to vitiate consent. An absence of consent in Alabama is defined in limited terms to occur where a person is coerced by the use of force, or threats of injury, or where the person is incapacitated as a result of the acts of the accused.[99] A person is deemed incapable of consenting only if they are younger than 16 years old, mentally defective, mentally incapacitated, or physically helpless.[100] The definition does not require 'freely given consent' or 'affirmative consent' and does not expressly encompass situations where the complainant is deceived as to the nature of conditions of the act. It follows that stealthing, and similar instances of deception, are unlikely to be prosecuted under the current state of law in Alabama.

On the other hand, in the state of California, the law of consent encompasses an 'affirmative consent' model. Affirmative consent is

95 *R v Lawrance* EWCA Crim 971.
96 Ibid.
97 Ibid.
98 *Violent Crime Reduction Act 2006* (UK); Crown Prosecutors Service (n 90) ch 6.
99 *Ala Code* § 13A-6-70(b).
100 Ibid § 13A-6-70.

where both sexual partners expressly indicate that they agree to continue with the sexual activity that is currently occurring.[101]

Under this iteration of consent, it is possible that victims of stealthing may have a cause of action under California consent law. As California's statutory definition of consent requires 'positive cooperation in an act' and because 'the person must act freely and voluntarily and have knowledge of the nature of the act or transaction involved', stealthing victims may argue that the accused took off the condom during sex and the victim was unaware of this until after the act.[102]

However, much like the current position in Australia, affirmative models of consent alone are considered insufficient to prosecute stealthing offences.[103] Affirmative consent reflects the view that a party must freely, voluntarily, and intelligently agree to the nature of the sexual act. In the case of stealthing, it is accepted that the victim has agreed to protected intercourse with the perpetrator; however, it is posited that the conditions of the act change when the accused removes the condom. Section 261.6 of the *Cal Penal Code* defines consent in terms of 'freely and voluntarily and have knowledge of the nature of the act or transaction involved'.[104] Accordingly, it is unclear whether, under these provisions, a victim's original consent is vitiated upon the removal of the condom as the nature of the act arguably remains the same.

It is considered that the introduction of 'conditional consent' as in the United Kingdom, may assist in prosecuting stealthing offences in these jurisdictions.[105] Under a model of conditional consent, the determinative factor of consent would be the 'material conditions' upon which consent was given rather than the 'overall nature' of the act.[106] Therefore, if courts in the United States utilised a conditional consent standard this might allow stealthing to be prosecuted as vitiating consent to sexual intercourse.[107]

International legal status of stealthing

Stealthing and similar instances of 'protection deception' have been the subject of judicial consideration internationally. Different perspectives

101 Melissa Blanco, 'Sex Trend or Sexual Assault?: The Dangers of "Stealthing" and the Concept of Conditional Consent' (2019) *Penn State Law Review* 123(1) 217, 228.

102 Ibid 229.

103 Ibid 239.

104 *Cal Penal Code* § 261.6.

105 Blanco (n 98) 217, 239.

106 Ibid.

107 Ibid.

on the legal status of stealthing and similar offences provide guidance and support for the treatment of stealthing. Other international judicial authority pertaining to stealthing and similar offences reveals that these offences have not been treated in a uniform manner.

In April 2021, New Zealand successfully prosecuted its first stealthing case.[108] The accused was found guilty of raping a sex worker in a Lower Hutt brothel. Prior to and during the sexual intercourse the accused was made aware that he was legally required to wear a condom and agreed to use one whilst at the brothel. The accused and complainant first had consensual sex with a condom, but when they had sex again, the accused removed the condom. The complainant indicated to the accused that he had acted inappropriately and made him put the condom back on. The accused then proceeded to remove the condom without the complainant's knowledge and ejaculated inside of her. Upon realising that the condom had been removed, the complainant ran to her manager's room and called the police.

Judge Stephen Harrop commented that sex workers were no less victims than any other survivor.[109] He also rejected the accused's defence that his actions were not premediated and that cultural factors were relevant to the sentencing, being the accused's recent arrival in New Zealand from the Philippines. Judge Harrop commented that the accused was told multiple times of the requirement to use a condom and that '[he] can't proceed on the basis that raping sex workers is any more acceptable [in the Philippines] than it is here'.[110] The accused was sentenced to three years and nine months' imprisonment.

A first-of-its-kind case was also prosecuted in Germany in 2018, where the accused was found guilty of sexual assault.[111] In this case, the accused carried out the stealthing offence at his apartment, after the complainant explicitly requested that the accused wear a condom. The complainant stated that she only realised that the man had not been wearing a condom when the accused ejaculated. The accused defended himself by stating that the condom had already ripped, prompting him to remove it completely and also claimed he ejaculated outside of the

108 Brianna Chesser, 'New Zealand's First Successful "Stealthing" Prosecution Leads the Way for Law Changes in Australia and Elsewhere', *The Conversation* (Article, 28 April 2021) https://theconversation.com/new-zealands-first-successful-stealthing-prosecution-leads-the-way-for-law-changes-in-australia-and-elsewhere-159323.

109 Ibid.

110 Ibid.

111 Matthew Robinson, 'Police Officer Found Guilty of Condom 'Stealthing' in Landmark Trial', *CNN* (Article, 20 December 2018) https://edition.cnn.com/2018/12/20/health/stealthing-germany-sexual-assault-scli-intl/index.html.

victim's body (an assertion denied by the victim). The accused was ultimately found guilty of sexual assault and was not found to be guilty of rape because, while the court found his act of 'stealthing' to be non-consensual, the sexual intercourse itself was deemed to be consensual.

Such a decision would not have been possible prior to the 2016 set of reforms in Germany which removed the antiquated requirement that complainants demonstrate that they physically resisted attacks before charges of rape and sexual and assault could be made.[112] Despite this decision, stealthing remains a grey area as the accused is the first person to be convicted of the offence in Germany.

International reform

Beyond the courts, lawmakers have supported the criminalisation of stealthing in the US. In response to Brodsky's (2017) article,[113] a group of American lawmakers banded together to urge that stealthing be classified as rape. Democratic representatives from US states including California and New York have corresponded with the House Judiciary Committee urging its members to address stealthing by criminalising it as rape.[114]

In October 2021, California became the first US State to outlaw stealthing under civil law.[115] The legislative reform makes it a civil offence under Californian state law to remove a condom without consent, by classing the act of stealthing as one of battery.[116] This allows victims to seek damages from the perpetrator under the state's civil code but does not result in incarceration or other criminal penalties.[117] Assemblywoman Christina Garcia has tried and failed on two previous occasions to pass a law criminalising the act.[118]

In addition to the recent criminalisation of stealthing in the ACT, Stealthing has also received legislative attention in other Australian states and Territories. In November 2020 the New South Wales Law

112 Ibid.
113 Brodsky (n 3) 183.
114 Maya Oppenheim, 'US Lawmakers Want "Stealthing" Classified as Rape', *Independent* (Article, 5 October 2017) www.independent.co.uk/news/world/europe/man-remove-condom-sex-stealthing-no-conviction-rape-consent-switzerland-lausanne-a7729656.html.
115 Holly Honderich and Shrai Popat, 'Stealthing: California Bans Non-Consensual Condom Removal' *BBC* (11 October 2021).
116 Ibid.
117 Ibid.
118 Brianna Chesser, 'In an Australian first, Stealthing is now illegal in the ACT. Could this set a Precedent for the Country?' *the Conversation* (12 October 2021).

Reform Commission (NSWLRC) suggested changes to the state's legislative regime. Along with the proposed introduction of a communicative model of consent, the NSWLRC suggested that stealthing should be a criminal offence. It was recommended that sex with a condom be legally defined as a specific activity that can be consented to, without consenting to any other sexual activity, such as sex without a condom.[119]

International perspectives provide guidance for the treatment of stealthing. *Assange* and *R(F) v DPP & A* demonstrate that common law jurisdictions have accepted that consent can be provided on the condition of condom usage or withdrawal prior to ejaculation.[120] If this condition is communicated and is disregarded, the accused's actions may attract liability for rape. Moreover, criminal legislation in ACT, Australia now includes intentional misrepresentations regarding condom use as one of the circumstances that is capable of negative consent. However, it is unclear whether these principles would be adequate to protect all stealthing complainants in all jurisdictions. These principles appear only to extend liability where the complainant has communicated this condition and the accused has deliberately disregarded it. It is evident that the principle needs to be comprehensive enough to cover circumstances where such a conversation has not occurred.

Stealthing as a tort

One view of the appropriate legal status of stealthing is to classify it as a tort. In her article, Brodsky (2017) suggested that stealthing might be best treated as a battery tort on the basis of liability for offensive, but not physically harmful, touch.[121] Brodsky (2017) ultimately proposed the introduction of a new tort specific to condom removal.[122] This would prohibit the removal of a condom during sex without the 'affirmative permission' of both partners. Brodsky (2017) opts for a tort model, as it would accommodate for both compensatory and punitive damages, which she views as the most appropriate remedies to address the varied harms of stealthing.[123] While it is possible that stealthing could be classified as a tort, a tortious remedy is rejected for a number of reasons.

119 New South Wales Law Reform Commission (NSWLRC), *Consent in Relation to Sexual Offences*, Report No 148 (2020) 68.

120 Athena Katsampes, 'A Rape by Any Other Name? The Problem of Defining Acts of Protection Deception and the University as a Solution' (2017) 24(3) *Virginia Journal of Social Policy & the Law* 157.

121 Brodsky (n 3) 183.

122 Ibid.

123 Ibid.

Firstly, compensation claims by way of tort have been viewed as a complicated method of redress for complainants.[124] Barriers that impede complainants might include limitation periods and the high costs and delays of litigation.[125] Furthermore, damages may not be the most appropriate remedy for the harm suffered by complainants of stealthing. For example, in most jurisdictions, damages work to compensate the plaintiff for loss suffered as a result of the tort; the plaintiff is entitled to be put in the position they would have been had the tort not been committed (*restitutio in integrum*).[126] Remedies under tort law would thus allow complainants of stealthing to seek financial damages from an offender. However, monetary compensation may be viewed as an unsatisfactory response to the non-financial damage which has stemmed from the sexual assault.[127]

Various authors have also expressed concern about the increased role that plaintiffs are likely to play in tort proceedings relating to sex offences.[128] This may expose them to defences like contributory negligence or 'risks of costs' orders. Sawyer and Tian (2009) fear that this may separate complainants into classes of 'more or less responsible for their own harm'.[129] Furthermore, with this increased involvement, plaintiffs in cross-examination may face the possibility of re-traumatisation. Another downfall is one which Brodsky acknowledges herself. Creating a discrete tort for non-consensual condom removal may isolate our understanding of the harm suffered by complainants.[130] If the sexual wrong of stealthing were rectified via civil remedy, society might perceive stealthing as a wrong less severe than other sexual offences shielded by the criminal law. As discussed, this construction of sexual offending is essential to reflect society's concern about this form of harm and to assist the complainant's recovery, and an isolated civil wrong may downplay their experience.

Thus, while alternative remedies in tort may provide monetary compensation for complainants of stealthing, the law of tort is insufficient to provide proper relief and deterrence. Various authors have similarly

124 ALRC (n 23).

125 Christine Forster, 'Good Lore or Bad Lore? The Efficacy of Criminal Injuries Compensation Schemes for Victims of Sexual Abuse: A New Model of Sexual Assault Provisions' (2005) 32(2) *University of Western Australia Law Review* 264, 272.

126 *Livingstone v Rawyards Coal Co* (1880) 5 App Cas 25, 39 (Lord Blackburn).

127 Richard Sawyer and Tom Tian, 'Negligent Sexual Assault: Reform of the Criminal Law and a Tort Alternative' (2009) 4 *The Journal of Law and Social Justice* 113, 120.

128 Ibid.

129 Ibid.

130 Brodsky (n 3) 183.

concluded that tort law is inappropriate to deal with the breadth of protection deception.[131] Plunkett (2014) views that imposing damages against accused persons in these classes of sexual violence is unlikely to provide adequate deterrence.[132]

Birth control sabotage

While academic and judicial discussion on the legal status of stealthing is limited, there is an abundance of discussion on the legality of the similar offence of birth control sabotage. Contraceptive sabotage occurs where there is deceptive interference with any form of protection or contraception performed with an intent to cause pregnancy.[133] This encompasses acts designed to make contraception ineffective, such as 'poking holes' in a condom or interference with contraceptive pills.[134] In 2014, the Canadian Supreme Court in *Hutchinson* ruled on the issue of consent in relation to contraceptive sabotage.[135] In this case, the complainant consented to sexual intercourse with the accused, under the condition that he use a condom to prevent pregnancy. Unbeknownst to the complainant, the accused poked holes in the condom prior to intercourse, with the intention of impregnating the complainant. The complainant became pregnant as a result of the intercourse, and the appellant was charged with sexual assault. The trial judge found that the complainant had not consented to sexual intercourse, and this was upheld on appeal to the Supreme Court of Canada. The majority found that the complainant had initially consented to sexual activity under the relevant legislation, but this consent was vitiated by fraud. The minority of Abella and Moldaver JJ instead took the view that the complainant had never consented to sex in the first place, stating at [98]:

> When individuals agree to sexual activity with a condom, they are not merely agreeing to a sexual activity, they are agreeing to how it should take place. [...] By any definition, when someone uses a condom, it is part of the sexual activity. It is therefore part of what

131 Katsampes (n 116) 157; Leah A Plunkett 'Contraceptive Sabotage' (2014) 28(1) *Columbia Journal of Gender and Law* 97, 102.

132 Ibid.

133 Ibid.

134 *R v Hutchinson* [2014] 1 SCR 346.

135 Ibid.

> is – or is not – consented to. And if what is consented to is sexual activity with a condom, the condom is expected to be intact. If it is not intact because of its deliberate sabotaging, the activity that has been agreed to has been unilaterally changed by the saboteur.

Such a view of condom-protected sex would likely consider that the deliberate removal of the condom without the individual's consent would also transform the act into sexual intercourse without consent. The criminalisation of contraceptive sabotage has been heavily supported by scholars, particularly in the American context.[136] Two scholars have proposed separate statute models that criminalise birth control sabotage in the United States.[137] These models support the treatment of the similar scenario of stealthing as a criminal offence.

Should stealthing be a crime?

At the moment, the *Crimes Act* in the ACT, Australia is the only legislation in any jurisdiction that explicitly identifies stealthing as a sexual offence. The treatment of stealthing and similar offences by the courts internationally however further supports the proposition that stealthing is criminal behaviour and should be deemed a criminal offence. *Hutchinson* and *Assange* support that the courts have accepted that consent can be provided on the condition that sex will be protected and that any violation of that condition subsequently vitiates consent.[138]

While the treatment of stealthing as a tort is valid, it is not the most appropriate means of addressing the harm caused to the complainant. We therefore propose that the appropriate legal avenue for condemning non-consensual condom removal lies in reform to the criminal law of consent. Such an approach is consistent with the recent reform in Australia.

136 Plunkett (n 127) 97, 102; Trawick (n 30) 721; Jed Rubenfeld, 'The Riddle of Rape by Deception the Myth of Sexual Autonomy' (2013) 122 *The Yale Law Journal* 1372; Ann Moore, Lori Frohwith, and Elizabeth Miller, 'Male Reproductive Control of Women Who Have Experienced Intimate Partner Violence in the United States' (2010) 70(11) *Social Science & Medicine* 1737; Nickeitta Leung, 'Education Not Handcuffs: A Response to Proposals for the Criminalization of Birth Control Sabotage' (2015) 15 *University of Maryland Law Journal of Race, Religion, Gender & Class* 146.

137 Plunkett (n 127) 97, 102; Trawick (n 30) 721.

138 Katsampes (n 116) 157.

Proposed reform: a conclusion

As the law currently stands, it appears uncertain whether non-consensual condom removal during sex will be considered to vitiate consent. This will largely turn on the approach taken by the courts in interpreting the current legislative provisions. Even where stealthing could conceptually vitiate consent due to fraud, the present provisions are not broad enough to encompass all instances of stealthing, particularly where the preference of condom use has not been expressly communicated. What is clear is that the criminal law surrounding consent must be altered to ensure such an act is criminalised. The chapter proposes that the introduction of an express statutory provision which establishes stealthing as a crime will address the inadequacies apparent under the current criminal legislation.

Criminal redress for stealthing

The criminal justice system is essential for responding to, and denouncing, sexual offending.[139] In a criminal trial, the state is represented as the adversary of the accused, and thus criminal offences are viewed as a harm against the state rather than an individual.[140] Criminalisation of stealthing thereby reinforces that stealthing is a societal problem and not a private civil matter to be dealt with between parties,[141] bringing the law into line with community values and deterring future incidents. The criminal law can provide remedies beyond monetary compensation by regulating human behaviour. Criminalising an offence importantly provides for societal condemnation, sending the message to accused persons that their behaviour is reprehensible.[142] The accused may also, in some circumstances, face the risk of incarceration, protecting complainants and deterring future acts.[143] This would also aid in the complainant's recovery by providing them with a sense of justice.

Stealthing as a criminal offence

This chapter ultimately proposes two possible options for criminalising stealthing. Firstly, it suggests creating a novel offence that would act as a stand-alone addition to current legislation. For example:

139 *Criminal Law Review* (2015), Department of Justice and Regulation (Vic), Victoria's New Sexual Offence Laws 6.
140 Fileborn (n 22) 7.
141 Trawick (n 30) 721.
142 Ibid.
143 Ibid.

Stealthing (1) A person commits an offence if –

(a) He or she intentionally sabotages or removes a condom before or during sexual intercourse without the express permission of the other person; and

(b) He or she lacks a reasonable belief that the other person would not consent to sexual intercourse without a condom.

A separate criminal model addressing stealthing, however, also presents fundamental flaws. The separation of stealthing from classical formulations of rape and sexual assault may have a negative effect on complainants, with the unintended consequence that complainants may feel as though their experience is less serious than other sexual assaults. Stealthing is, as put by Brodsky, 'rape adjacent', where any artificial segmentation may further obfuscate our understanding of the offence and may create an unintended distinction between sexual offences and stealthing.[144] This may reinforce the stigma that 'deceptive sex, however bad it may be, isn't that bad'.[145] An alternative proposal would be to include stealthing as an offence under the current consent provisions. This involves including stealthing in the list of circumstances that vitiate consent, meaning that an individual would be regarded as not consenting if another person, during intercourse, removed the condom without their express permission.

For example, criminal acts or codes that provide a list of circumstances where a person is not consenting could be altered to include the following provision:

(1) Circumstances in which a person does not consent to an act include, but are not limited to, the following –

    (a) Where the condom/contraceptive device is removed without the express permission of the other.

This is similar to the approach recently adopted in the ACT, which includes an intentional misrepresentation about condom use as one of the circumstances that is capable of negating consent.[146] However, as noted above, the ACT legislation requires a representation to be made about condom use. For this reason, our recommend wording is preferred.

144 Brodsky (n 3) 183, 209.
145 Rubenfeld (n 132) 1372, 1416.
146 *Crimes Act 1900 (ACT)* s 67(1)(h).

Effect of criminalisation

Under either of these proposed provisions, consent would be vitiated where a person intentionally removes the condom without the other person's express permission. This encompasses an individual removing a condom without their sexual partner's consent without restricting the gender or sexuality of either party. The requirement of express permission promotes the free and voluntary agreement model of consent, which requires a positive and willed action. Furthermore, these models allow for the offence to be recognised despite an initial consent to sexual intercourse. These provisions expressly recognise that any initial consent is nullified where the condom is removed without consent. Thus, in cases where the jury finds that these certain facts exist, consent will be irrefutably considered to be absent.

Criminalising stealthing as a separate offence may well create difficulties with complainant vocabulary and has the potential to diminish the importance of the offence. As discussed previously, there also remain issues with the mens rea of the offence, for example, distinguishing between intentional, and/or reckless/accidental removal.[147] Furthermore, the criminalisation of any offence presents the possible experience of re-traumatisation which may occur during the trial process.[148]

Final comments

Non-consensual condom removal, or stealthing, is a dangerous sex crime which has become increasingly prevalent in society. The legal status of such an act depends on whether stealthing is deemed to vitiate consent to sexual intercourse, and without any case law on the subject, its future treatment is uncertain. Such an act could vitiate consent, as it changes the condition of the act an individual has consented to, thereby requiring fresh consent for the act to validly continue. While stealthing arguably vitiates consent, its classification as rape is dependent on the court's interpretation of the current legislative provisions relating to consent. We therefore propose two alternative legal provisions to reform

147 Leung (n 132) 146, 161.
148 Criminal Justice Sexual Offences Taskforce (n 2) 910.

the current statutory provisions to unequivocally designate stealthing as a criminal offence. Ultimately, the introduction of a separate statutory provision is endorsed, as it appropriately separates stealthing from the existing offences and avoids the confusion of adding to an already convoluted area of law.

4 Desire-based contracting, BDSM, and consent

Introduction

Volenti fit non injuria – to a willing person no injury be done

The ideas and arguments in this chapter arose out of the realisation that consent is not binary, nor is it applied as a legal concept equally for men and women, straight and queer. Further, that women who are subjected to violence in their relationships are not supported if they choose to remain in that relationship, particularly if they are considered an active participant in that dynamic, however that is construed. And that feminists and feminist approaches to these issues render such realisations in a binary, rigid, and absolute way that arguably leaves no room for women who do not subscribe to 'acceptable' feminist understandings of what the 'right' relationship is for women.

The Latin phrase at the beginning of this chapter is an old Roman dictum that still forms a basic legal principle in contemporary Western legal systems. Consent is central to many criminal and civil laws, particularly around personal physical integrity. This chapter will focus on consent as it is understood and relevant to both sexualities and bodily integrity using the lens of bondage, discipline, and sadomasochism (BDSM).

The academic landscape within which many studies of bondage, discipline and sadomasochism (BDSM) reside is a confluence of sociology, philosophy, criminology, law, psychology, psychiatry, and gender, queer, and sex theories. The practice of BDSM is not widely studied and most literature situates BDSM in contexts specific to one of the above-mentioned areas. Authors tend to focus on the desirability (or not) of the practice of BDSM, particularly in relation to the assumed harm BDSM may cause individuals and society more broadly, and the majority of discussion centres around this issue.

DOI: 10.4324/9781003165606-4

This chapter aims to examine the relationship between BDSM, particularly the practices of sexually dominant men with sexually submissive women, feminism, consent, and the criminal law. An examination of the literature reveals a number of themes in the current work and each theme links with others, creating a complex and somewhat circular literature setting. The most noticeable aspect of the literature is the absence of the voices of BDSM practitioners, with notable exceptions, particularly women, who enjoy sexual submission with a dominant male partner, and sexually dominant men who enjoy sex with 'submissive' women. These two groups form the core focus of research currently underway.

The literature explored in relation to this chapter falls into three main thematic groups, all of which overlap and integrate, but can be identified in the following way:

1. Feminisms: including the historical viewpoints of women within Second Wave and now Third Wave feminist activism and discussion,
2. Consent: to assault and sexual activities, the framing of consent and the ways it is negotiated and known, and
3. Law: particularly the legal principles relating to consent to bodily harm and sexual intercourse, and the introduction of family violence legislation.

Each of these themes will be discussed in this chapter, and it will become clear that BDSM is considered a controversial and multifaceted sexual practice and vibrant subculture that challenges 'mainstream' feminist understandings of 'good' sex, 'good' relationships, and 'good' feminism. The practice of BDSM by women provides a lens through which to explore these themes and how the regulation of female sexuality and sexual expression occurs, even, and perhaps especially, within feminist discourse.

Some notes on terminology

Each of the three key subject areas considered in this chapter – BDSM, feminism and the criminal law – has specific terms that need a short introduction, and the choice of certain terms is significant.

BDSM

Bondage, discipline, and sadomasochism (BDSM) is an umbrella term for a range of sexual practices characterised by the infliction or receipt of pain, binding a person using various methods, and/or psychological domination and submission.[1] This study will use the acronym 'BDSM' to encompass the majority of labels used.

Femsub/Dom

This chapter will adopt the term 'femsub' to describe women who engage in sexually submissive roles with 'dominant' or 'top' men in a BDSM context. This term is used within the BDSM community to describe this role as both a noun and a verb.[2] Additionally, 'Dom' will refer to a man who enjoys sexually dominant roles.[3]

Feminisms

The diversity of feminist positions regarding specific issues such as pornography, sexuality, BDSM, and gender identity means that it is both inaccurate and confusing to refer to 'radical' versus 'liberal' feminism any longer as individuals can identify in different ways. 'Radical' feminism was, at one time, used to describe those who advocate for women's sexual liberation; however, self-identified 'radical' feminists such as Andrea Dworkin and Diana Russell were vehement opponents of BDSM and the term is now far less clearly defined.[4]

Sex-positivism is an inclusive position 'encompass[ing] a wide variety of sexual behaviours, sexual identities and gender identities that are traditionally viewed as deviant'.[5] Sex-positivity was embraced by 'liberal' feminists in the 'sex wars' of Second Wave feminism who viewed sexuality as inherently healthy and diverse.[6] While all sex-positive feminists are not proponents of BDSM, they take the position that denouncing a

1 See, e.g., Gloria Brame et al, *Different Loving: The World of Sexual Dominance and Submission* (Villard, 1993); D J Williams, 'Different (Painful) Strokes for Different Folks: A General Overview of Sexual Sadomasochism (SM and its Diversity)' (2006) 4(13) *Sexual Addiction & Compulsivity* 333; Jay Wiseman, *SM101: A Realistic Introduction* (Greenery Press, 2nd ed, 1996).

2 Alex Dymock, 'But Femsub Is Broken Too! On the Normalisation of BDSM and the Problem of Pleasure' 3(1) (2012) *Psychology & Sexuality* 54.

3 Brame et al (n 1); Wiseman (n 1).

4 Andrea Dworkin, *Pornography: Men Possessing Women* (Plume, 1981); Gayle S. Rubin, *Deviations: A Gayle Rubin Reader* (Duke University Press, 2011).

5 K. Paige Harden, 'A Sex-Positive Framework for Research on Adolescent Sexuality' (2014) 9(5) *Perspectives on Psychological Science* 455, 457.

6 Ann Russo, 'Conflicts and Contradictions among Feminists over Issues of Pornography and Sexual Freedom' (1987) 10(2) *Women's Studies International Forum* 103.

woman's sexual preferences is anti-feminist and aligns with conservative patriarchal views regarding the control of women's sexuality.[7]

The terms 'anti-BDSM' and 'sex-positive' feminism will be used throughout this chapter in place of 'radical' and 'liberal' feminism to clarify and define these positions. Non-binary gender is not addressed in this chapter, not because it has no place in BDSM but because the focus of this chapter is the legal mirroring of a heterosexual Dom/femsub relationship in domestic violence law. The BDSM community is incredibly diverse and comprises a range of sexualities and genders that are not captured in this short chapter.

What is BDSM?

BDSM is described by Brame et al (1993) as 'a thoughtful and controlled expression of adult sexuality that holds the promise of intense intimacy and sharing'.[8] The term 'sadomasochism' (SM) was first used by Sigmund Freud at the turn of the twentieth century and is a 'portmanteau noun created by conflating the words "sadism" [...] and "masochism"'.[9] It is widely associated with the Marquis de Sade (the 'father' of sadism – the taking of pleasure from the infliction of pain) and the novels of Leopold von Sacher-Masoch (the namesake of masochism – the taking of sexual pleasure through feeling pain).[10]

'Bondage' and 'discipline' are essentially sexual practices within the sadomasochistic sexual subculture.[11] Brame et al (1993) describe bondage as 'the sensual experience of safe captivity. To be in bondage is to have no options but to accept one's physical helplessness'.[12] Wiseman (1996) provides a more concrete definition: '[p]hysical materials applied to a submissive to restrain their ability to move'.[13]

Discipline is defined by Wiseman (1996) as '[t]raining by a dominant in how they wish their submissive to behave. Also, the punishment and correction administered by the dominant when the submissive fails to act in the proper manner'.[14]

7 Johanna Schorn, 'Subverting Pornormativity: Feminist and Queer Interventions' (2012) (37) *Gender Forum* 15.
8 Brame et al (n 1) 5.
9 Theodore Bennett, 'A Polyvocal (Re)Modelling of the Jurisprudence of Sadomasochism' (2012) 36(2) *University of Western Australia Law Review* 199.
10 Ibid; Brame et al (n 1); Gary W. Taylor and Jane M. Ussher, 'Making Sense of S&M: A Discourse Analytic Account' (2001) 4(3) *Sexualities* 293.
11 Wiseman (n 1).
12 Brame et al (n 1) 206.
13 Wiseman (n 1) 368.
14 Ibid 370.

The core elements of BDSM sexual practice, as opposed to other sexual practices, are the application of pain in a sexual context and the exchange of power, that is, a deliberate and often profound inequality in the power dynamics of those engaging in the 'scene', or BDSM session.[15] Typically, a BDSM practitioner will adopt a role that denotes power or the lack of power – that is, dominant or submissive roles. Roles are not gendered and may be assumed by any person, regardless of gender identity, sexuality, age, or physicality.[16] There are a variety of terms used to describe these roles such as Master or Mistress, slave, sub, Bull, piglet, bitch, Top and bottom. Note the capitalisation of dominant role names.[17]

Additionally, and perhaps most importantly for the purposes of this chapter, BDSM is, and must always be, explicitly consensual.[18] This is in counterpoint to the difficulties surrounding consent discussed in relation to the crime of stealthing, as discussed in Chapter 3. The negotiation and knowledge of consent in the BDSM subculture is intricately outlined and often prepared in the form of a contract. This will be discussed in detail later in this chapter.

Pathologising BDSM

BDSM is broadly considered a deviant and problematic sexual preference by many in the medical and legal professions and this view persists in mainstream culture.[19] BDSM has 'frequently been characterised as a disorder', and 'associations have been made between sadism, rape and murder [...] and sadism and child abuse'.[20] The depiction of BDSM in psychiatric literature is generally negative, with an emphasis on the harm BDSM fantasies and practice do to the practitioner and their sexual partner/s.[21]

15 Taylor and Ussher (n 10) 293; Williams (n 1) 333.

16 Katherine Martinez, 'BDSM Role Fluidity: A Mixed-Methods Approach to Investigating Switches within Dominant/Submissive Binaries' (2017) 65(1) *Journal of Homosexuality* 1.

17 Wiseman (n 1).

18 Brame et al (n 1); Taylor and Ussher (n 10) 293; Williams (n 1) 333; Wiseman (n 1).

19 Ummni Khan, 'Sadomasochism in Sickness and in Health: Competing Claims from Science, Social Science, and Culture' (2015) 7(1) *Current Sexual Health Reports* 49; Martinez (n 16) 1; Williams (n 1) 333.

20 Jonathan Powls and Jason Davies, 'A Descriptive Review of Research Relating to Sadomasochism: Considerations for Clinical Practice' (2012) 33(3) *Deviant Behavior* 223.

21 For a comprehensive discussion, see Khan (n 19) 49.

This negative view of BDSM and BDSM practitioners as deviant, sick, and harmful to themselves and others pervades the way BDSM is depicted in mainstream media as a reflection of societal views.[22] An interest in BDSM is often used as evidence of criminality and perversion in the law and forensic psychology/psychiatry.[23] Comprehension of why BDSM is sought out by psychologically healthy women appears to elude many in the health and legal professions, and this chapter aims to provide evidence for the development of that understanding.

Legal practitioners, and judicial officers, in particular, grapple with BDSM in profound ways. Reported legal cases involving BDSM are few, and most pertain to a fatality and a corresponding murder or manslaughter charge which supports the common view that BDSM is dangerous, violent, and to be denounced.[24] This pervading view of BDSM as harmful and a practice to be discouraged by the legal fraternity is framed by Bennett (2012, 2015) as 'lacking both a compelling theoretical basis and a practical rationale'.[25] Further discussion of BDSM and the criminal law is undertaken later in this chapter.

Feminisms

The 'sex wars' – feminism and sadomasochism in the 1970s and 1980s

The beginning of sadomasochism (SM), or BSDM, as a political movement can be traced back to the 1970s. Political BDSM 'emerged in the aftermath of the civil rights, sexual liberation, women's liberation and gay and lesbian liberation movements, from which it borrowed language, ideas and a sense of entitlement to equal treatment'.[26]

Women's participation in BDSM, particularly as submissive partners, developed into a deeply controversial issue within Second Wave feminism and was one of the issues, along with pornography, that caused the division within feminism that came to be known as the 'sex wars'.[27] Much of the literature produced during the sex wars refers

22 Khan (n 19) 49.

23 Theodore Bennett, 'Persecution Or Play? Law and the Ethical Significance of Sadomasochism' (2015) 24(1) *Social & Legal Studies* 89.

24 See *R v Brown* [1994] 1 AC 212; *R v Stein* [2007] 18 VR 376; *R v Wilson* [1996] 3 WLR 125.

25 Bennett (n 23) 89.

26 Rostom Mesli and Gayle Rubin, 'SM Politics, SM Communities in the United States' in David Paternotte and Manon Tremblay (eds), *The Ashgate Research Companion to Lesbian and Gay Activism* (Ashgate Publishing, 2015) 291.

27 Gayle S. Rubin, 'Blood under the Bridge: Reflections on "Thinking Sex"' (2011) 17(1) *GLQ: A Journal of Lesbian and Gay Studies* 15.

specifically to lesbian BDSM given heterosexual BDSM was fundamentally problematic from any feminist viewpoint at that time. Men dominating women sexually was seen to be abusive and an extension of the misogyny of the prevalent patriarchal norms that it was simply not discussed by feminists at that time, beyond a general reiteration that a woman's sexual expression was her own choice.[28]

Indeed, BDSM was situated by anti-porn feminists in the same category as pornography, both profoundly 'woman-hating' and misogynistic.[29] Further, sadomasochistic pornography was touted as 'mainstream' pornography and an illustration of how anti-woman and inherently degrading pornography is. Feminist anti-pornography campaigners such as Andrea Dworkin and Diana Russell used BDSM pornography as an illustration of the inherently misogynistic character of porn, without acknowledging that not all pornography, or even most pornography, objectively contained BDSM content.[30] There is an argument that could be made in the current age of the mainstreaming of hardcore and violent pornography that this position carries a lot more weight,[31] but in the 1970s and 1980s mainstream pornography was, in comparison, relatively tame.[32]

Much of the literature examining BDSM, particularly that written in the 1980s and early 1990s, specifically addresses this tension within feminism – is BDSM 'anti-woman' and 'anti-feminist'? Or is it sexual empowerment and female sexual expression at its most fundamental?[33] Given the only BDSM discussed at this time, beyond heterosexual BDSM depicted in pornography, was lesbian BDSM practice, it is to be presumed that only lesbian women were entitled to publicly pose this question about their sexuality.[34] As a fundamental tenet, anti-porn feminist discourse and theory sees male dominance as inherently problematic and insidious, and a woman willingly seeking out masochistic experiences at the hands of a man is to be pitied as a brain-washed

28 Gayle S. Rubin, 'Thinking Sex: Notes for a Radical Theory of the Politics of Sexuality' in Carol S. Vance (ed) *Pleasure and Danger: Exploring Female Sexuality* (Routledge and Kegan Paul, 1984) 267; Russo (n 6) 103.

29 Janice Winship, 'Pornography, Men Possessing Women. Andrew Dworkin (Book Review)' (1982) 11(3) *Feminist Review* 97.

30 Rubin (n 27) 15.

31 Melinda Tankard Reist and Abigail Bray *Big Porn Inc: Exposing the Harms of the Global Pornography Industry* (Spinifex Press, 2014).

32 Rubin (n 28) 267.

33 Marie France, 'Sadomasochism and Feminism' (1984) 1(16) *Feminist Review* 35; Russo (n 6) 103.

34 Patrick D. Hopkins, 'Rethinking Sadomasochism: Feminism, Interpretation, and Simulation' (1994) 9(1) *Hypatia* 116.

slave,[35] not considered transgressive and liberated.[36] Even sex-positive feminists at this time considered heterosexual, particularly Dom/femsub BDSM, as troubling.[37]

From an anti-BDSM feminist standpoint, such as that adopted by Dworkin and Jeffreys, BDSM should be viewed as a form of 'self-harm' and the 'result of oppressive forces such as sexual abuse, bullying, physical violence, hatred and contempt'.[38] While taking a somewhat less condemnatory stance, France argues that 'feminist sadomasochists share the same fascination with power and gratification as capitalist patriarchs',[39] but that BDSM is 'a reaction to living under patriarchy, not a reflection of it'.[40]

From the literature, it is clear that anti-BDSM feminism views BDSM as objectionable on three main grounds:

1 BDSM, even lesbian BDSM, replicates and furthers patriarchal relationships and patriarchal power structures,
2 Consent to activities which eroticise dominance, submission, pain, and powerlessness is the result of internalised misogyny and cannot be trusted, and
3 BDSM is simply sexualised violence dressed up as erotic game-playing and is no different from non-consensual sexual violence.

Each of these grounds underpins a theme in the literature – the 'true nature' of BDSM as 'power sex', the authenticity of consent, and the characterisation of BDSM by the law and large parts of society as violence rather than sexual practice. Each theme will be discussed in greater detail below.

The 'truth' about BDSM

One of the most vehemently argued positions taken by anti-BDSM feminists, on the one hand, and sex-positive feminists, on the other, is

35 Rubin (n 27) 15; Russo (n 6) 103.
36 France (n 33) 35; Elisa Glick, 'Sex Positive: Feminism, Queer Theory, and the Politics of Transgression' (2000) 64(1) *Feminist Review* 19.
37 See, for a general discussion, Hopkins (n 34) 116; Mesli and Rubin (n 26) 291; Rubin (n 28) 267.
38 Shelia Jeffreys 'Body Modification as Self-Mutilation by Proxy' in Viv Burr and Jeff Hearn (eds), *Sex, Violence and the Body: The Erotics of Wounding* (Palgrave Macmillan, 2008) 15, 30.
39 France (n 33) 35, 41.
40 Ibid 40.

whether BDSM is a replication and extension of male violence against women and the misogynistic patriarchy in which women are suppressed. Anti-BDSM feminists consider consensual BDSM as a fallacy and symptomatic of the internalised misogyny women who engage in BDSM suffer.[41] France differs in this view somewhat, in that she argues that BDSM is a *reaction* to living in a patriarchal culture, not a reflection of it per se.[42] However, her representation of BDSM as an undesirable sexual practice aligns with the anti-BDSM feminist stance.

Hopkins attempts to address the issues raised by anti-BDSM feminists by arguing that BDSM 'does not replicate patriarchal sexual activity. It simulates it'.[43] Hopkins posits that BDSM practitioners are not merely 'reproduc[ing] patriarchal activity in a different physical area', but that they 'selectively replay surface patriarchal behaviour onto a different contextual field'.[44]

This theory seeks to position BDSM as more nuanced and psychologically layered than anti-BDSM feminists portray it and invites a deeper understanding of BDSM as more than just the powerful hurting the vulnerable for sexual gratification. Hopkins places BDSM amid the political, the individual, even the psycho-sexual, and wants us to understand the subtleties of BDSM that anti-BDSM feminism does not acknowledge.

There are, of course, issues with Hopkins's view. Firstly, the pain inflicted by Dominants or Tops on their submissive partners is real, not just a 'simulation'. As Bennett (2015) argues,

> pain and physical hurt really do occur as a result of sadomasochistic practice; sadomasochists are not like actors using 'blunted blades', sadists actually whip, flog and cane masochists, and masochists end up actually bruised and cut.[45]

The fact that BDSM practices involve *actual* bondage, pain, and humiliation renders Hopkins' description of BDSM as mere 'fantasy' and 'simulation' somewhat inaccurate and naive. Stear (2009) is also critical of Hopkins's approach, noting that 'Hopkins' idea of simulation is largely mechanical', and that his theory 'relegates the psychological

41 Dworkin (n 4).
42 France (n 33) 35.
43 Hopkins (n 34) 116.
44 Ibid.
45 Bennett (n 23) 89.

dimension to the side-lines when this is, in fact, central' to the emotional and erotic experience of BDSM.[46]

The concept that BDSM can be reduced to a mere game is also somewhat inadequate as a description of BDSM practice. While Stear (2009) invokes Kendall Walton's theory of 'make-believe', a model Walton uses to describe our engagement with art, film, and theatre,[47] this characterisation of what can be a profoundly emotional and deeply affecting erotic (and psychological) experience is one-dimensional. As Califia writes in her review of the BDSM and leather culture book *Hard Corps*,[48]

> SM sex is consensual: it meets the same needs for sexual gratification and psychological balance that other kinds of sexuality fulfil for other people; its elements of dominance and submission are no more stringent than those of organised religion, and its ritualised encounters no more inflexible than the institution of marriage, and there is more often than not a great deal of trust and affection between SM participants.[49]

It seems, then, disingenuous and simplistic to render BDSM practice as only a simulation of violent sex or erotic game-playing. Practitioners consider it a lifestyle and a community, even a profound experience, rather than just a sexual game.

Neither Stear's nor Hopkins's 'explanation' for BDSM really cuts to the heart of *why* a feminist woman would *choose* to be a masochist, bottom, or submissive to a man. It is the 'why' that seems to render the act either acceptable or unacceptable in feminist theory. Sex-positive feminists would argue that, if her motivation is based in empowerment and autonomy, if she comes from a place of sexual freedom and agency, then her choice to engage in masochistic sex reflects the most fundamental feminist values of equality and freedom.[50] If her motivation is based in fear and coercion, then we are no longer talking of BDSM but abuse, the 'true' nature of BDSM in the anti-BDSM feminist approach.

46 Nils-Henne Stear, 'Sadomasochism as Make-Believe' (2009) 24(2) *Hypatia* 21, 29.

47 Ibid.

48 M Grumley and E Gallucci, *Hard Corps: Studies in Leather and Sadomasochism* (Dutton, 1977).

49 P Califia, 'Hard Corps: Studies in Leather and Sadomasochism' (1978) 3(3) *Journal of Homosexuality* 301.

50 Ummni Khan, 'A Woman's Right to Be Spanked: Testing the Limits of Tolerance of S/M in the Socio-Legal Imaginary' (2008) *SSRN Electronic Journal* 1. https://doi.org/10.2139/ssrn.1255022.

This logical progression leads into the next theme in the literature: consent.

Contextualised consent

Consent has been a rallying cry of Second and Third Wave (and arguably First Wave) feminism, a core message that 'No Means No' and women's right to say no is, or should be, inalienable and absolute.[51] However, it is notable that, '[d]espite its utter simplicity and apparent reasonableness, supporters of "no means no" are still having to make their case on a daily basis', and that 'many still believe that a woman's outright verbal rejection of sexual advances' does not mean she is not consenting.[52]

This statement is supported by the Australian National Research on Women's Safety (ANROWS) *National Community Attitudes towards Violence against Women Survey* (NCAS), conducted three times in the last decade. This important initiative gives a snapshot of community attitudes to gendered violence longitudinally. The most recent NCAS report in 2018 found that changes in attitudinal support for violence against women were relatively small over that time.[53] In order to gauge attitudinal support for violence against women, questions that propose excusing perpetrators of violence against women, disregarding the need to gain consent, minimising violence against women, and mistrusting women's reports of violence were put to respondents. The answers to those questions gave each respondent a score in each section.[54]

Relevant to this discussion, the percentage of male survey respondents in the section on 'disregarding women's right to consent' who agree with the statement 'Women often say "no" when they mean yes' supports Little's assertion. Fully 14% of male respondents agreed with this statement, as did 11% of the women.[55] Further, 24% of male respondents agree with the statement 'Women find it flattering to be *persistently* pursued, even if they are not interested' (emphasis added),

51 See, e.g., Germaine Greer, *The Female Eunuch* (McGraw-Hill, 1970); Catherine A. MacKinnon, *Feminism Unmodified: Discourses on Life and Law* (Harvard University Press, 1987).

52 Nicholas J Little, 'From No Means No to Only Yes Means Yes: The Rational Results of an Affirmative Consent Standard in Rape Law' (2005) 58(4) *Vanderbilt Law Review* 1321, 1322.

53 Craig Webster and Molly Klaserer, 'Fifty Shades of Socialising: Slosh and Munch Events in the BDSM Community (2018) *Event Management* 23(1) 135–147.

54 Ibid.

55 Ibid 27.

as did 13% of female respondents.[56] Lastly, 30% of men and 27% of women surveyed agreed with the statement 'When a man is very sexually aroused, he may not even realise that the woman doesn't want to have sex.'[57] That is, approximately one in three men and more than one in four women surveyed held the view that male sexual arousal is potentially uncontrollable.

The NCAS results align with other surveys conducted in comparable countries. For example, the End Violence Against Women Coalition, a British organisation, commissioned a survey of nearly 4,000 participants on attitudes to sexual consent.[58] The results indicated that about one-third of male respondents did not think pressuring a woman to have sex was 'rape' unless there was physical violence.[59]

In her analysis of consent literature, Beres found that '[e]ven within the literature on sexual consent there is no consensus on what it is, how it should be defined or how it is communicated'.[60] It can be argued that the 'lack of empirical work on the communication of willingness and "consent" to sexual relations'[61] Beres found in 2007 has not been greatly expanded in 2021, despite the considerable interest in this area since the #MeToo movement began. The discussion of consent, and specifically how we know what it is, has not moved far beyond 'I know it when I see it'.

As discussed in Chapter 2, the legal definition of consent can be loosely described as either 'free and voluntary agreement' or 'consent freely and voluntarily given'.[62] And there is no statutory definition of consent in Australia at this time that goes beyond these phrases (see s2A *Criminal Code Act 1924* (Tas) for example). Recent attempts to define consent more narrowly and reverse the onus of consent from the woman to the man (the heteronormative drafting of criminal law is a topic for another publication but must be noted as inherently problematic) has resulted in concepts such as 'communicative' and 'enthusiastic' consent.[63]

56 Ibid.

57 Ibid.

58 YouGov, *Attitudes to Sexual Consent* (Research Report, December 2018) www.endviolenceagainstwomen.org.uk/wp-content/uploads/1-Attitudes-to-sexual-consent-Research-findings-FINAL.pdf.

59 Ibid 2.

60 Melanie Beres, '"Spontaneous" Sexual Consent: An Analysis of Sexual Consent Literature' (2007) 17(1) *Feminism & Psychology* 93, 94.

61 Ibid.

62 Australian Law Reform Commission (ALRC), *Family Violence – A National Legal Response,* Report No 114 (2010) 1150.

63 See, e.g., James Monaghan and Gail Mason, 'Communicative Consent in New South Wales: Considering Lazarus v R' (2018) 43(2) *Alternative Law Journal* 96.

Certainly, within broader feminist discourse and BDSM culture, consent is not well defined and is the subject of much internal debate. Anti-porn/BDSM feminist discourse considers even explicit consent as suspect and a product of the 'sexual oppression of women' in a patriarchal society.[64] This form of feminism sees sexual practice through the lens of power and oppression, and women's 'submission' as the only logical response to this oppression.[65] Consent cannot be given freely, in this understanding of patriarchal culture, and is therefore not authentic consent at all. Concepts such as 'communicative' and 'enthusiastic' consent have no meaning in this paradigm as anti-porn/BDSM feminists reject that consent can be given by a woman to a man *at all.*

The sex-positive feminist considers that female desire and sexual expression have been repressed by mainstream patriarchal attitudes to women and the control of women's reproductive rights and sexual expression outside marriage.[66] Sex-positive feminists see consent as a vital and powerful element of women's sexual liberation, but it is, on the whole, ignored in the discussions of women's sexual repression. A woman's consent is both powerful and authentic in the sex-positive framework and many sex-positive feminist authors give great weight to freedom of consent.[67] This approach effectively renders discussion about a woman's consent authenticity moot as it is assumed that a woman has the agency and autonomy to freely consent (or not) to sex.

However, both positions accept the concept that consent is a satisfactory framework within which to consider willing, or otherwise, participation in sexual activity. A notable exception is Brown (1995), who asserts that '[c]onsent [...] marks the presence of power, arrangements, and actions that one does not oneself create but to which one submits'.[68] Brown (1995) makes the compelling argument that consent 'functions as a sign of legitimate subordination' because it 'involves agreeing to something the terms of which one does not determine'.[69]

64 Russo (n 6) 103, 107.

65 See, e.g., Dworkin (n 4); MacKinnon (n 51); Diana Russell, 'Sadomasochism: A Contra-Feminist Activity' (1982) in Robin Ruth Linden, Darlene R. Pagano, Diana E. H. Russell and Susan Leigh Star (eds), *Against Sadomasochism: A Radical Feminist Analysis* (Frog in the Well, 1983) 176.

66 See, e.g., Glick (n 36) 19; Rubin (n 28) 267; Russo (n 6) 103.

67 See, e.g., Khan (n 50); C Queen, 'Sex Radical Politics, Sex-Positive Feminist Thought, and Whore Stigma' in B Ryan (ed), *Identity Politics in the Women's Movement* (New York University Press, 1997), 92–102.

68 Wendy Brown, *States of Injury* (Princeton University Press, 1995) 162.

69 Ibid 163.

Further to Brown's objections to the acceptance of the 'consent framework' is the broader problem of the continued acceptance of the false narrative that men propose sexual activity and women consent to it. This narrative does not provide for the broad range of sexual practices, relationships, contexts, and negotiations, nor does it provide room for homosexual or queer sexual practices.[70]

This disjunction between the theory of binary consent and the reality of human sexual attitudes and experience is not well researched. Beres's literature review of consent research exposes a conspicuous gap in the knowledge and understanding of how consent is known, how it is expressed, and when it is important or relevant.[71] The nature of discourse in Western societies around consent has been, to date, problematic, as the results of the surveys mentioned above show. 'Mainstream' feminist arguments that consent is either present or not, have not been universally accepted, and the feminist rhetoric in response has been that there is something wrong with individuals who challenge the consent binary, or with the society they live in and are part of.[72]

In an effort to cross this divide between 'no means no' and 'sometimes no means yes', binary consent has been developed into more nuanced approaches such as 'communicative consent', 'enthusiastic consent', and 'affirmative consent' legislation.[73] Communicative consent was first proposed as an alternative to traditional 'no means no' consent models in 1989 by Pineau in her essay on date rape.[74] Describing it as a 'deliberate form of consent', she argued that it 'moves the responsibility of consent from women [...] onto men to demonstrate that they obtained women's consent'.[75] Proponents of 'communicative consent' argue that this is a more evolved version of the 'yes means yes' approach.[76]

The New South Wales criminal trial of *Lazarus* triggered a substantial review to that state's criminal laws with regard to sexual consent, with other states following shortly behind.[77] The defendant in that matter, Luke Lazarus had his conviction for sexual assault overturned

70 Robin Bauer, *Queer BDSM Intimacies* (Palgrave Macmillan UK, 2014).

71 Beres (n 60) 93.

72 See, e.g., T D Latimour (2013). *When Should 'Yes' Mean 'No'? Informed Consent to Sexual Activity, Mistake, and the Role of the Criminal Law* [Bachelor of Laws dissertation, Honours, University of Otago]. Dunedin, New Zealand; Little (n 52) 1321; Diana Russell, *Making Violence Sexy: Feminist Views on Pornography* (Open University Press, 1993).

73 Beres (n 60) 93; Latimour (n 72); Monaghan and Mason (n 63) 96.

74 Beres (n 60) 93.

75 As cited in Beres (n 60) 93, 102.

76 Bauer (n 70); Monaghan and Mason (n 63) 96.

77 *Lazarus v R [2016]* NSWCCA 52.

on appeal. His retrial resulted in acquittal and appeared to turn on the narrow issue of the defendant's knowledge as to whether the victim was consenting.[78]

The issue of consent in *Lazarus* turned on the victim's evidence that she had not consented and had communicated this to the accused, but also, and perhaps more importantly in the context of consent jurisprudence, on the circumstances of the alleged incident. The following facts were accepted by the courts in both trials:

- The victim was intoxicated, though the level of impairment was at issue,
- The accused was also intoxicated,
- The accused and victim had met only minutes before on a crowded dance floor,
- The accused had essentially tricked the victim to accompany him into an alley out the back of the nightclub, and
- The accused had engaged in anal intercourse with the victim without lubrication or preparation.[79]

It was the Crown's contention that the court should find that these circumstances were such that a reasonable person would have turned their mind to the possibility that the victim was not consenting. These were apparently risky circumstances involving two intoxicated strangers, a dark alley, and objectively painful sexual intercourse without discussion or preamble. For the court to find that the accused was reasonable in his assumption that the victim was consenting is objectively bizarre. This is after the court rejected the victim's version that she said, 'no' and 'stop' several times, leaving the court with a version of events still so problematic on its face that the verdict caused understandable public uproar and triggered a change in NSW consent law to require 'communicated consent'.

The *Lazarus* case highlights the difficulties of the consent binary. Ignoring the victim's version of events leaves the court with a set of circumstances that may or may not indicate a lack of consent. The court essentially turned itself in knots in finding that consent was not given but that the accused reasonably believed it was. This is not a legal construction but a reality of human sexual encounters in Western society. Perhaps, the issue is not 'was there consent' but 'why did the court not

78 *R v Lazarus* [2017] NSWCCA 279.

79 Joseph Briggs and Russ Scott, '"Rape Myths" and a "Reasonable Belief" of Consent R V Lazarus [2017] NSWCCA 279' (2020) 27(5) *Psychiatry, Psychology and Law* 750.

accept the victim's version of events'. This speaks to a much deeper issue with the use of adversarial trials to resolve allegations of sexual assault and is a discussion for another publication.

Alternatives to consent frameworks

Conceptualising non-consent as a simple 'no means no' has its problems. Despite the rising understanding of men's sexual violence against women, no corresponding drop in *actual* violence against women has occurred in Australia and comparable countries.[80] In reality, countries such as Denmark and Sweden, objectively considered progressive and safe places for women to live and work, have some of the highest rates of sexual violence against women in the world.[81] The 'Nordic Paradox', as it has been termed, gives pause when considering the effectiveness of the binary consent framework, and this chapter aims to explore different approaches used by BDSM practitioners that work beyond 'consent'.

Sex-positive feminists such as Rubin (1984) argue that 'there are deep problems with the political discourse of consent'[82] and that anti-BDSM feminism essentially entrenches the 'legal regulation of sexual conduct'.[83] Sex-positive feminism holds that attempts to legislate sexual practices inevitably lead to 'legalized moralism' whereby 'deviant' sexual practices are considered non-consensual and coercive, to be denounced and criminalised for the good of wider society.[84] From the sex-positive position, all laws pertaining to sexual conduct, other than sexual assault laws, should be abolished, and the authenticity of consent be respected when it is freely given.[85]

If this view of consent is accepted, there appears no need to define consent beyond 'free agreement'. A person's willingness, or otherwise, to engage in a particular sexual practice is to be accepted without attempt to subvert it or look beyond it to construct reasons to undermine it. However, this view ignores the social context of the giving and negotiating of consent, the power imbalances inherent in most sexual encounters by virtue of gender, age, sexuality, social status, and race (to name a few). It is once again relying on the binary of consensual or

80 Webster and Klaserer (n 53) 135–147; YouGov (n 58).

81 EIGE. (2015). *Gender Equality Index 2015: Measuring Gender Equality in the European Union 2005–2012 (Country Profiles)*. European Institute for Gender Equality.

82 Rubin (n 4) 175.

83 Ibid 166.

84 Ibid 165.

85 Glick (n 36) 19; Khan (n 50) 1.

non-consensual, without reference to desire or pleasure and the reality that 'consensual' sex can also be harmful if it is not pleasurable.

Conversely, within the BDSM subcultural context, it appears from the limited research undertaken to date that desire and pleasure are fundamentally entwined with understandings of consent for BDSM practitioners. In his study of the negotiation of consent amongst 'dyke+ queer' BDSM practitioners, Bauer (2014) found that ' "[r]eal" abuse was not arousing to [practitioners], which underlines the significance of social context for the meaning of actions'.[86] While rape and abuse fantasies are relatively common within BDSM practice, it is the consensual nature of playing out those fantasies in a BDSM context that is a vital part of that play.[87]

For some BDSM practitioners, such simulations of abuse are considered 'healing', 'transformative', and a way of reframing past trauma in ways that give them back control and agency. For players in this space, BDSM is a powerful way to 'reframe' past sexual trauma and intimate partner violence in a safe and highly controlled environment.[88] Consent is 'the defining characteristic of BDSM and distinguishe[s] it from violence, abuse, rape, oppression [...] with which it is often associated'.[89]

This framing of consent in BDSM as mutually agreed and based on desire and pleasure necessitates a relatively sophisticated model of negotiation based on communication. BDSM practitioners emphasise the importance of open and frank communication between 'play partners'.[90] Indeed, several systems have been developed to assist this communication such as the 'traffic light' code words of red, orange, and green; safe words; and 'checking in'.[91] Many BDSM practitioners engage in lengthy discussions with prospective partners before engaging in sexual play, including the use of checklists and non-sexual meetings

86 Bauer (n 70) 77.

87 Ibid; Dossie Easton, 'Shadowplay: S/M Journeys to Our Selves' in Darren Langdridge and Meg Barker (eds), *Safe, Sane and Consensual: Contemporary Perspectives on Sadomasochism* (Palgrave Macmillan, 2007) 223.

88 For discussion, see Meg Barker et al, 'The Power of Play: The Potentials and Pitfalls in Healing Narratives of BDSM' in Meg Barker and Darren Langdridge (eds), *Safe, Sane and Consensual: Contemporary Perspectives on Sadomasochism* (Palgrave Macmillan 2007, 2013) 197; Easton (n 87) 223; Cheryl A. Renaud and Sandra E. Byers, 'Positive and Negative Cognitions of Sexual Submission: Relationship to Sexual Violence' (2006) 35(4) *Archives of Sexual Behavior* 483.

89 Bauer (n 70) 77.

90 Ibid; Morten Nielsen, 'Safe, Sane, and Consensual – Consent and the Ethics of BDSM' (201) 24(2) *International Journal of Applied Philosophy* 265; Wiseman (n 1).

91 Wiseman (n 1) 52–57 for discussion on safe words.

to discuss each other's needs and preferences.[92] This is 'communicative consent' in its most evolved iteration.

The authenticity of a femsub's consent

When discussing consent and BDSM more broadly, the nagging question at the heart of those who are not interested in, or practicing, BDSM, is *why* would anyone *want* to be hurt, bound, or humiliated? This question also underpins the justice system's response to BDSM and the legal concept of consent.

As mentioned previously, one of the central arguments of anti-BDSM feminists is that a submissive or masochistic woman's consent to BDSM practices, such as spanking, caning, flogging, and bondage, is entirely inauthentic and untrustworthy, as women's desires are merely products of the misogynistic culture in which they were raised. The anti-BDSM feminist argument renders enthusiastic female participation in 'deviant' sex as akin to 'Stockholm Syndrome' and evidence of impaired mental health.[93]

However, this assumption seems to be entirely based on a position that it is not rational or reasonable that a woman – or any person – would *enjoy* being 'hurt' or 'violated,' and would even seek out so-called 'violent sex.' As Ritchie and Barker summarise, '[t]he common SM discourse of consent is of little weight with feminists who feel that this made it worse: that women deliberately seek out situations where they could be powerless victims due to internalised hatred'.[94]

Russo (1987) explores this from a more conflicted position as a self-described 'radical lesbian feminist' and a woman who has 'never felt comfortable nor secure in even thinking about these issues'.[95] Russo describes being 'accused of being male-identified and anti-feminist' by anti-porn/BDSM feminists when she 'tried to understand and clarify the "pro-sex" position'.[96] This outright dismissal of women who practice and enjoy BDSM as 'male-identified' and suffering from 'internalised misogyny' characterises the attacks on BDSM and pornography during the sex wars.[97]

92 Bauer (n 70).

93 Jeffreys (n 38) 15; Russell (n 72).

94 Ani Ritchie and Meg Barker, 'Feminist SM: A Contradiction in Terms or a Way of Challenging Traditional Gendered Dynamics through Sexual Practice?' (2005) 6(3) *Lesbian and Gay Psychology Review* 227.

95 Russo (n 6) 103, 104.

96 Ibid.

97 Lal Coveney et al, *The Sexuality Papers* (Hutchinson, 1984); Dworkin (n 4); MacKinnon (n 51); Russell (n 65) 176.

This antagonism by anti-BDSM feminists towards then-called 'anti-anti-porn' or 'pro-sex' feminists is described by a number of writers in the 1980s.[98] A woman's consent to anything other than presumably heteronormative, or perhaps only lesbian, sex is highly suspect according to anti-porn/BDSM feminist theory,[99] and anti-BDSM feminists consider any woman who claims to enjoy and pursue BDSM as brain-washed and self-hating.[100]

What, then, *is* the experience of self-identified feminist women who engage in the submissive or masochistic role in BDSM? Research into women involved in BDSM is scarce and to date no research has focused on women who enjoy sexually submissive BDSM play with male sexually dominant partners.

Two studies specifically focusing on women in BDSM were identified: Ritchie and Barker (2005), and Bauer (2014).[101] Ritchie and Barker conducted focus group-based research with a small group of self-identified feminist BDSM-practicing women. All of the women identified as bisexual or lesbian and over half also identified as predominantly submissive or 'bottoms'.[102] Bauer's research involved 'dyke+queer' BDSM practitioners, both male- and female-identifying participants. As the nomenclature suggests, all participants identified as queer, lesbian, gay, or trans, and Bauer focused on the way consent is negotiated by his interview partners in his research.[103]

The dialogue recorded by Ritchie and Barker is insightful and illuminates the lived experience of feminist women BDSM practitioners. When asked about anti-BDSM feminist theories, the participants expressed confusion that anti-BDSM feminists consider BDSM anti-feminist, pointing to the prevalence of female Dominants/Tops and male submissives/bottoms as evidence that BDSM can be empowering for women.[104]

Further, the participants challenged the assumption by anti-BDSM feminists that the femsub has no power or control and is subject to abuse or potential abuse. One of the participants stated,

> even if it is [a] woman sub, [there's an assumption] that subs don't have any kind of power and it's more complicated than that [...] You

98 Califia (n 49) 301; Mesli and Rubin (n 26) 291; Rubin (n 27) 15.
99 France (n 33) 35.
100 Russo (n 6) 103.
101 Meg Barker et al (n 88) 197; Bauer (n 70).
102 Ritchie and Barker (n 94) 227.
103 Bauer (n 70).
104 Ritchie and Barker (n 94) 10.

> *do* have a certain amount of power as the bottom in the scene, part of its power you're sort of giving over to the top, but it's not [...] it's a lend.[105]

The anti-BDSM feminist argument that BDSM replicates and reinforces a heteronormative, violent sexual culture is strongly rejected by the participants in Ritchie and Barker's study. One participant described BDSM as 'enabling men to cry and experience vulnerability' and described being 'a woman who penetrates rather than is penetrated'.[106] Another participant dismissed the concept that any relationship could be without power imbalances, 'arguing that just isn't borne out in reality'.[107] Indeed, Ritchie and Barker assert that BDSM renders power dynamics more visible, more honestly, than 'vanilla' sexual relationships.[108] Participants also pointed out that, in BDSM, power is not connected to privilege, particularly in relation to gendered hierarchies of power.[109]

Bauer's participants spoke of negotiated consent and the role social context and heteronormative gender performance play in influencing understandings of consent outside the BDSM dynamic. As all the participants identified as 'dyke+queer', the participants in this research spoke mainly from a position eschewing heteronormative sexual dynamics, but their views regarding the core requirement of consent in all play were strongly held, nuanced, and clear.[110]

While both studies involved small groups of women, the opinions and experiences of these women, who all offer meaningful and insightful narratives, cannot be discounted. These opinions and experiences are echoed by other feminist BDSM practitioners, including Pat (now Patrick) Califia and Gayle Rubin, who both led the sex-positive feminist movement in the sex wars. The idea that a woman's consent, especially a woman who is well-versed in feminist theory and dogma, and who calls herself a feminist, is untrustworthy is offensive and patronising to them.[111]

As a result of heteronormative mainstream views of consent and women's sexuality, as well as conservative political moves to regulate women's bodily autonomy and reproductive choice, the anti-BDSM

105 Ibid 11, emphasis in original.
106 Ibid 12.
107 Ibid.
108 Ibid 13.
109 Ibid.
110 Bauer (n 70).
111 Califia (n 49) 301; Rubin (n 4).

feminist view of consent has been adopted in the law of Western countries. 'No means no' is not only encapsulated in law, it is only recently that 'yes means yes' has been included as well.

However, consent is not only relevant in the context of sexual activity within the criminal law. The broader concept of bodily autonomy gives rise to well-established legal concepts of consent to physical touching of any kind and the principle that a person cannot consent to being injured or harmed. This legal principle is at odds with the Latin legal phrase that begins this chapter, *Volenti fit non injuria*, but is confirmed in case after case, with exceptions that appear to defy logic at first glance.

BDSM and consent at law

As in the United Kingdom, Australian law as it currently stands renders consensual touching that causes actual bodily harm unlawful and amounting to assault. At law, the absence of consent turns a lawful act (sexual intercourse or touching) into an unlawful assault. There is some difference between Code states (those with criminal law based on criminal codes, such as Western Australia and the Australian Capital Territory) and common law states (those whose law has been developed through case law and custom, such as New South Wales and Victoria) as to the requirements to prove assault and the nuances of the application of those laws; however, the result is generally the same.[112]

For example, in New South Wales, section 61 *Crimes Act 1900* (NSW) simply states that assault is an offence. No further definition of assault is given. This is because some crimes, such as 'goods in custody', 'larceny' (stealing), and 'assault' were imported from Great Britain as 'common laws' and have been legislated in the most basic form as the elements and definitions of these offences lie in historical case law. As set out in several cases in which certain decisions decided the law regarding particular parts of the offence, the elements of common assault in New South Wales are:

1 The accused struck or touched, or threatened to strike or touch, the victim/complainant,
2 intentionally,
3 without consent, and
4 without lawful excuse.[113]

112 Bennett (n 9) 199.
113 Ray Watson, *Criminal Law (NSW)* ed GS Hosking, AM Blackmore, and R Watson (LBC Information Services, 1996).

For the purposes of the discussion of the law of assault here, it is not useful to go into the cases that established the four elements of assault, nor the rationale underpinning the reasons for those decisions. The offence of common assault is the least serious of the various forms of assault in that no injury needs to have been caused. In Australia, the general rule is that the seriousness of the assault charged is contingent on the seriousness of the injury caused. This is not always true, however, as in cases of attempted murder or shoot with intent to murder – for those offences, no injury need be inflicted for a finding of guilt.

The elements of assault are fairly universal across Australia, with only minor differences in state jurisdictions. On the face of it, then, it appears that BDSM practice that causes no injury is lawful. However, Bennett, in analysing the various laws that may affect BDSM practitioners, asserts that the legal situation is far more complex and problematic.[114]

The law in Australia states that a person cannot consent to actual bodily harm – that is, any injury that is 'calculated to interfere with the health or comfort of the [victim]. Such hurt or injury need not be permanent, but must, no doubt, be more than merely transient or trifling'.[115] Bruising, red marks that lasted several hours, and welts have all been held to be actual bodily harm.[116]

The legal rule that one cannot consent to injury is set out in the so-called Spanner Trials, known at law as *R v Brown* [1994] 1 AC 212. This case is problematic in contemporary Australian society for several reasons that will be examined below.

In this case, a group of gay men who had been engaging in BDSM activities for over ten years together, were prosecuted by the Crown for assault. The group of men were of differing ages (an aggravating factor in the court's view), were experienced and engaged in a range of BDSM practices including bondage, flogging, cutting, caning, 'cock and ball torture', and anal sex. The alleged injuries inflicted on the submissives included piercing of penises with nails (although this was in reality a nail pushed through a pre-existing genital piercing), bruising and abrasions caused by flogging and beating, and cutting scrota with scalpels.[117]

The victims/defendants (most of the group were both charged with inflicting injuries on others and aiding and abetting injuries inflicted by others on themselves) gave evidence that they fully and freely consented

114 Bennett (n 9) 199; Bennett (n 23) 89.

115 *R v Donovan* [1934] 2 KB 498;(1936) 25 Cr App R 1.

116 Watson (n 113).

117 Chris White, 'The Spanner Trials and the Changing Law on Sadomasochism in the UK' (2006) 50(2–3) *Journal of Homosexuality* 167, 169–170.

to the injuries inflicted on them and obtained pleasure from the experience.[118] Despite this, the court found the accused men guilty after their attempts to have the consent of the 'victims' accepted by the court failed. The case proceeded on appeal to the Court of Criminal Appeal and later the House of Lords, where the appeal was denied. The case serves as the basis for law in Australia that a person is not able to consent to bodily injury.

R v Brown has been extensively analysed and discussed, both in the context of sadomasochism and sexual bias,[119] and in the more general context of consent to assault at law.[120] The issues raised in the case are still controversial in that the decision was not strictly based in law but was made on policy grounds, the Court of Criminal Appeal finding that 'it was not "in the public interest" to allow people to engage in such activities'.[121] The same court had, over the years and several different cases, found that certain activities were permissible 'in the public interest', including boxing, tattooing, contact sports, and piercing.[122]

White (2006) describes the reactions and comments of the Lords during the appeal:

> the Lords put forward a series of assertions and contentions that defined SM, not as erotic pain-play, but as violence [...] The Lords put forward an 'inevitable' connection between homosexuality and paedophilia, and the potential for an unpredictable escalation in violence. They conjured horrific pictures of brutality, of genital torture, degradation and humiliation, beating, wounding, blood-letting, and the smearing of human blood, with the putative connection between gay SM and AIDS.[123]

118 Ibid.

119 Sandeetha Chandra-Shekeran, 'Theorising the Limits of the "Sadomasochistic Homosexual" Identity in *R v Brown*' (1997) 21(2) *Melbourne University Law Review* 584; Marianne Giles, 'R v Brown: Consensual Harm and the Public Interest' (1994) 57(1) *Modern Law Review* 101; White (n 117) 167.

120 John Devereux, 'Consent as a Defence to Assaults Occasioning Bodily Harm – the Queensland Dilemma' (2003) 14(2) *The University of Queensland Law Journal* 151; Giles (n 119) 101; Cheryl Hanna, 'Sex Is Not a Sport: Consent and Violence in Criminal Law (Sadomasochism and the Law)' (2001) 42(2) *Boston College Law Review* 239; William Wilson, 'Is Hurting People Wrong?' (1992) 14(5) *The Journal of Social Welfare & Family Law* 388.

121 Cited in White (n 117) 167.

122 Ibid 170.

123 Ibid 175.

This apparent homophobic and arguably patently incorrect and prejudicial view of the defendant's conduct in the Spanner Trials is examined through a feminist lens by Chandra-Shekeran (1997), particularly when juxtaposed with the courts' approach to the issue of consent in allegations of heterosexual rape. While the Lords in *Brown* seemed incapable of imagining that a person *could* consent to the BDSM sex as described by the participants, Chandra-Shekeran posits that there is real resistance in the courts to the concept of consent as a threshold issue in *heterosexual* sexual assault allegations.[124]

Further, Chandra-Shekeran points out that the House refused to characterise the activities described in *Brown* as sexual and insisted on reading the BDSM play as violence.[125] This is in stark contrast to non-consensual heterosexual sex where the courts had, until that time particularly, refused to categorise non-consensual sex as violence. Citing Smart (1994), Chakra-Shekeran states, 'the *Brown* decision has left Britain with a law on sexuality which states – symbolically at least – that when women say "No" to rape they mean "Yes" but when men say "Yes" to homosexual sex they mean "No"'.[126]

Chakra-Shekeran's summary may seem outdated but negative legal attitudes to homosexual sex persist in contemporary Australian jurisprudence. While sodomy has been decriminalised across all jurisdictions in Australia and the UK since *R v Brown*, the so-called 'gay panic' partial defence of provocation to murder was still good law across Australia into the decade. South Australia, the first state to decriminalise homosexual sex, was the last to remove the 'gay panic' defence in 2020.[127] Essentially a version of the partial defence of provocation, the defence was available to an accused who had killed a person who made a homosexual advance on them, even if that advance was not violent nor persistent.[128]

This summation of the gendered and heteronormative application of the law of consent to assaults said to have occurred in the context of BDSM is borne out by several cases. In *R v Wilson* [1996] 2 Cr App R 241, the accused branded his initials into his wife's buttocks, at her request. He was initially charged with assault occasioning actual bodily harm and convicted. However, on appeal, the court overturned his

124 Chandra-Shekeran (n 119) 584.

125 Ibid 588.

126 Ibid 587.

127 Isabel Dayman, 'South Australia Becomes Final State to Abolish 'Gay Panic' Murder Defence', *ABC News* (Article, 2 December 2020) www.abc.net.au/news/2020-12-01/gay-panic-defence-abolished-by-sa-parliament/12940296.

128 See *Lindsay v The Queen* [2015] HCA 16; *Green v R* 334 (1997) CLR 191.

conviction, distinguishing the injuries inflicted from those inflicted in *Brown* by characterising the brands as 'tattooing'. The court referred somewhat obsequiously to the accused's 'desire [...] to assist [his wife in what she regarded] as the acquisition of a desirable personal adornment, perhaps in this day and age no less understandable than the piercing of nostrils'.[129]

Similarly, a female accused was charged with assault after caning her male partner's back and buttocks 25–30 times, leaving welts, bruising, and bleeding wounds. He reported the alleged assault to police as the relationship broke down, but the jury acquitted the woman after only 15 minutes' deliberation. The only defence asserted was that the caning was consensual, relying on the unchallenged evidence produced to the court of the couple's long history of BDSM play.

Indeed, it takes a very serious injury to result in conviction when the accused and victim are heterosexual and married, as in the above two cases. In *R v Emmett* [1999] EWCA Crim 1710, the accused was charged with two separate counts of assault occasioning actual bodily harm. The first count related to an incident where he nearly asphyxiated his fiancée to death during a consensual BDSM session when he left a plastic bag on her head too long. She sustained haemorrhaging in her eyes from oxygen deprivation. The second count arose from a second-degree burn she sustained when he poured lighter fluid on her breasts and lit it. The victim gave evidence she consented to the activities, and it was the evidence of her doctor that resulted in the charges.

The court in *R v Emmett* felt compelled to convict the accused, citing the 'serious' burn that must have been 'excruciatingly painful' for the victim. It also cautioned against erotic asphyxiation, pointing out the 'grave danger of brain damage, or even death'.[130] However, despite the extent of the injuries inflicted, the accused received a suspended sentence, meaning he was not imprisoned immediately, for two years. By comparison, the defendants in the *Spanner Trials* received between one and four and a half years' imprisonment each for inflicting injuries objectively far less serious.

There is a clear inference to be drawn that heterosexual couples engaging in what is arguably dangerous sex play with an objectively high risk of death or serious permanent injury will be treated less harshly by the courts than homosexual men engaging in choreographed and controlled sadomasochistic play. No one was being set on fire or asphyxiated in the play described during *R v Brown*, yet every defendant went to

129 *R v Wilson* [1996] 3 WLR 125, 244.
130 *R v Emmett* [1999] 1710 EWCA Crim, 6.

prison. The Lords in *Brown* railed against the activities, the 'sadomasochistic homosexual' identity, the dangers of not only sadomasochism but *gay* sadomasochism, and denounced the defendants in thunderous tones of outrage. By contrast, their Honours in *R v Emmett* were considerably more circumspect, saying, 'it is plain, in our judgment, that the activities involved in by this appellant and his partner went well beyond that line [where consent becomes irrelevant]'.[131]

It is important to note the differences in the way courts deal with homosexual sadomasochism as opposed to heterosexual sadomasochism. Gender appears to play quite an important role in the attitude courts take to allegations of consensual actual bodily harm and informs the courts' approach to cases where the conduct is alleged to have occurred in the context of BDSM. It is open to argue that this attitude is reflected in the relative leniency shown in matters of heterosexual domestic violence.

It is clear from the judges' comments in *Brown* that non-heterosexual BDSM is considered far more deviant than heterosexual BDSM, even when the heterosexual relationship between the 'victim' and the accused is outside the preferred one of committed partnership or marriage. Rubin (2011, first published in 1984) asserts that a 'sex hierarchy' exists in Western societies and at the top of that hierarchy are heterosexual, married couples.[132] The sex practiced by these couples is 'Good'; it is reproductive, monogamous and 'holy'.[133] Homosexuals, people who are transgender, BDSM practitioners, and sex workers would then be seen to reside at the bottom of the hierarchy, engaging in 'Bad' sex, below unmarried heterosexual couples, promiscuous heterosexual men, then women, then monogamous gay and lesbian couples, and so on.[134]

Khan (2008) refers to Rubin's hierarchy in her analysis of two films featuring BDSM and asserts that BDSM practitioners can raise their sexual status on the hierarchy by conforming to heteronormative standards such as marriage, monogamy, and heterosexuality.[135] This hierarchical framing of sexuality appears to align with the judicial decisions in legal cases involving BDSM.

In *R v Stein*,[136] the defendants were a pimp, Peter Stein, and his prostitute girlfriend, Catherine Doolan. Doolan had been providing sexual services to the deceased, David Macdouall, for some time, and the two

131 *R v Emmett* [1999] 1710 EWCA Crim, 7.
132 Rubin (n 4).
133 Ibid 152.
134 Ibid.
135 Khan (n 50) 1, 30.
136 *R v Stein* [2007] 18 VR 376.

agreed to play submissives to Stein one night, for which Macdouall would pay $400. During the ensuing session, Macdouall died from asphyxiation as a result of being gagged.

Despite causing the death of the deceased by engaging in objectively dangerous (and non-consensual) conduct during a BDSM session, then driving the victim's body to a paddock several days later and burning it, Stein received a four-year sentence of imprisonment. This is in comparison to the sentences of one to four years given to the defendants in *Brown* for inflicting transitory harm on consenting adults.

It is reasonable to frame this disparity in sentencing within Rubin's sexual hierarchy: on the one hand, a socially deviant sexual context, but somewhat elevated in the hierarchy by the heterosexual nature of the situation, and on the other a socially deviant context that is ostensibly at the bottom of Rubin's hierarchy due to the homosexuality of the participants who are further penalised as a result.

In addition to a framing of judicial penalisation of deviancy, there appears to be a gendered application of penalty. Where women are either the victim or the accused, the courts invariably view the offence at the lower end of seriousness. While the victim and one of the co-accused in *R v Stein* were men, the scene was not homosexual in nature, and the involvement of Doolan appears to have mitigated Stein's culpability somewhat. As Chandra-Shekeran posits, '[the courts appear find it] necessary to produce a realm of unacceptable male-to-male behaviour and to maintain the boundaries of an "authentic" heterosexual space'.[137]

However, Chan and Gommer propose a different explanation for the inconsistencies in judicial findings and sentences.[138] Using biological theory of law, they assert that judicial officers react from a deep-seated 'biological imperative' and cases such as *R v Brown* challenge judges' moral and ethical views, eliciting emotional responses such as disgust and fear.[139] They also examine the differences in legal outcomes between *R v Brown* and *R v Wilson*, arguing that the moralistic and outraged language used by the judges in *Brown* was absent in *Wilson* because the judges considered Wilson and his wife as a heterosexual married couple, though somewhat deviant. The language in *Wilson* was measured and typical of a legal judgement because the judges view the Wilsons as

137 Chandra-Shekeran (n 119) 584, 593.

138 Erica Hei-Yuan Chan and Hendrik Gommer, 'Sexually Biased Case Law: A Biological Perspective' (2011) 7(4) *IJPS* 155.

139 Ibid 161–166.

part of the 'in-group' of socially desirable people, that is, heterosexual, married, and therefore entitled to privacy.[140]

On its face, *R v Wilson* appears to establish the legal principle that BDSM in the privacy of one's own home, that causes no injury beyond that which is 'merely transient or trifling', and that occurs between a heterosexual couple, preferably married, is lawful, even protected. However, Bennett sees this conclusion as flawed when the laws and decisions around manslaughter are taken into account.[141]

Bennett examines three known Australian cases of manslaughter, as charged, where the death of the victim was found to have occurred in the context of a consensual BDSM session. The cases Bennett discusses are *Q v Meiers* (Unreported, Supreme Court of Queensland Trial Division, Lyons J, 8 August 2008) in which a man suffocated to death while tied to a veranda post by his wife; *R v McIntosh* [1999] VSC 358 where a man died as a result of consensual erotic asphyxiation at the hands of his lover; and *R v Stein* (2007) 18 VR 376 in which the client of a prostitute and her pimp died when the handkerchief he was gagged with was not removed despite his apparent distress.

The deaths in each case were deemed 'accidental' in that the accused did not intend for the victim to die; however, the accused was found to have acted recklessly, or negligently, given the outcome. All three victims in these cases died by asphyxiation and Bennett points out that all three cases involved conduct that would, had the victims not died, not meet the threshold for prosecution. The act of temporarily restricting someone's airway with their consent does not ordinarily cause bodily harm and is therefore not apparently unlawful.[142] However, the judges in all three matters found that the recklessness or negligence of the accused as to the risk of death or serious injury was enough to meet the legal threshold for criminal conduct.[143]

This characterisation of otherwise lawful conduct as criminal in the context of BDSM relies heavily on the legal concept of recklessness. Bennett argues that this approach to BDSM by the courts creates a category of 'sadomasochistic assaults that become "unlawful" if they carry the risk of injury [...] the activity itself must be scrutinised to determine whether or not it is "risky"'.[144] In this way, Bennett considers that BDSM practitioners may be subject to prosecution for acts that do not

140 Ibid 164–165.
141 Bennett (n 9) 199.
142 Ibid 207.
143 Ibid.
144 Ibid 208.

cause bodily harm but *could have* done only because of the inherent riskiness of BDSM itself.

Conclusion

The position of BDSM practitioners in wider Australian society appears somewhat precarious given the uncertain legality of BDSM practice, particularly in the context of a greater understanding of intimate partner violence. The literature points to a clear bias or inequality in the application of consent law principles to cases involving BDSM, but there has been no research undertaken in Australia involving heteronormative BDSM-practicing couples regarding their understanding of, or response to, this legal jeopardy.

In addition, the role of feminism and Third Wave feminism's impact on contemporary sexually submissive women is not known. This is a significant gap in the research in this area and has interesting implications for the way women's sexuality and relationships with men are policed in a post-'#MeToo' environment. The 'sex wars' reflect contemporary discussions within feminist discourse, and this aspect of the literature is highly instructive when analysing current responses to BDSM from a feminist view.

The irony that BDSM practices regarding desire-based contracting can offer a far more nuanced and mature approach to consent jurisprudence while being effectively criminalised by 30-year-old legal precedent is profound. The discourse around consent continues to focus on the binary nature of the concept, despite the reality being, in the main, far less clearly defined. The 'rape myths' that underpin many legal decisions in sexual assault cases remain active, and the measured,[145] 'affirmative' approach to consenting to sexual activity between consenting adults offered by desire-based contracting would seem to provide a counterpoint to these myths. If the norm became frank discussion between adults about what they wanted to do with each other prior to engaging in sexual activity, even to the point of writing it down, issues of consent coming before a court would be clearer to adjudicate.[146]

It is clear from the poor performance of the criminal courts in providing a level of justice to sexual assault victims, and the lack of success seen in reducing the rate of intimate partner violence and intimate partner violence-related homicide across the world, that the current

145 Briggs and Scott (n 79) 750.
146 Bauer (n 70).

system is simply not working. The focus on a 'submissive' consent model leads to attempts by the system to distil complicated human motivations and actions into a simplistic 'yes' or 'no'.[147] This is not workable, and not working, and many lives are irreparably damaged as a result.

147 Brown (n 68).

5 Consent concluded?

Final remarks

The laws surrounding the concept of consent have evolved significantly since their earliest known iteration, where consent was seen as a violation to the property owned by a husband or father. However, the historical context of these laws and the perpetuation of rape myths continue to influence the contemporary formation of consent and impact the understanding of consent law in Western common law countries.

It was not until the mid-nineteenth century that the notion of 'consent' was developed as the distinguishing factor between lawful and unlawful sexual activity.[1] In most jurisdictions, the law recognises that rape and other sexual offences are grounded on a lack of consent, with points of divergence still existing surrounding the specifications of what entails consent. For example, laws vary in respect of requirements for positive resistance or regarding the perpetrator's knowledge of the victim's lack of consent.[2] Ultimately, most jurisdictions have advanced considerably from the common law understanding of rape as 'carnal knowledge' and have repealed once relevant principles such as the marital rape immunity.

The development of consent has been largely framed by both principles of liberalism and feminism – in particular, theoretical discussions about how the nature and scope of sexual offences fit in with recognised human rights, such as an individual's right to equality and privacy.[3] In fact, it is considered that all references to 'consent'

1 Simon Bronitt and Bernadette McSherry, *Principles of Criminal Law* (Thomson Reuters (Professional) Australia, 4th ed, 2017) 656.

2 Vanessa E. Munro, 'From Consent to Coercion" in Clare McGlynn and Vanessa E. Munro (eds), *Rethinking Rape Law: International and Comparative Perspectives* (Taylor & Francis Group) 17, 20.

3 Bronitt and McSherry (n 1) 638.

DOI: 10.4324/9781003165606-5

at international law must be interpreted in a manner consistent with human rights law standards.[4] An individual's sexual autonomy has been expressed as a core human rights value which provides the basis for the legal concept of consent.

Despite the importance of recognising the rights to privacy, equity, and sexual autonomy, it is also important that rights are balanced with their counterparts – for example, the need to alter the 'veil of privacy' in order to protect the vulnerable has been increasingly acknowledged.[5] This is contrasted with the concern that the desire to preserve an individual's liberty and right to privacy could result in dangerous forms of sexual activity remaining beyond the ambit of the law.[6] As discussed in Chapter 4, this debate has particularly arisen in the context of BDSM practices which challenge and extend the 'traditional' forms of consent to sexual activity.[7]

The definition of consent varies considerably from jurisdiction to jurisdiction in its scope and application. Some jurisdictions adopt an 'affirmative' model of consent which stipulates that a person must act freely and voluntarily and must have knowledge of the nature of the act.[8] While progressive, it is considered that affirmative models of consent are alone inadequate to protect complainants against the breadth of contemporary sex crimes, such as stealthing.[9] Accordingly, consent should also adhere to a 'conditional' model, which considers the 'material conditions' on which the consent is given as the determinative factor of consensual conduct.[10] Conditional models of consent have allowed for the successful prosecution of stealthing in the United Kingdom and ought to be adopted in other jurisdictions.

Consent laws also need to evolve beyond their current binary nature to overcome the present bias and inequality in the application of consent law principles. For instance, it is considered that the popular 'communicative' models of consent which reverse the onus of consent from

4 Amnesty International, 'Rape and Sexual Violence' (2011) *Human Rights Law and Standards in the International Criminal Court* (Report, 2 March 2021) www.amnesty.org/en/documents/IOR53/001/2011/en/.

5 See, e.g., Bronitt and McSherry (n 1) 638; Simon Bronitt, 'The Right to Sexual Privacy, Sado-masochism and the Human Rights (Sexual Conduct) Act 1994 (Cth) (1995) 2(1) *Australian Journal of Human Rights* 59.

6 Bronitt (n 5) 59.

7 Ibid.

8 Melissa Blanco, 'Sex Trend or Sexual Assault?: The Dangers of "Stealthing" and the Concept of Conditional Consent' (2019) *Penn State Law Review* 123(1) 217, 228.

9 Ibid.

10 Ibid.

the woman to the man, cannot operate effectively in light of our inherently patriarchal culture and society. An analysis of BDSM practices supports the adoption of a 'desired-based contracting' model which would allow for open discussions between adults about the conditions of their consent prior to engaging in sexual activity.

While there is no uniformity in definition there are several key themes that can be taken from the various international definitions of consent:

1 Consent should be explicitly conveyed and offered freely, including discussion around the material conditions on which consent is given;
2 Conditions of the sexual act should not be altered (e.g. removing condom) as this would require fresh consent; and
3 Legislation is clearer where circumstances where an individual is not consenting are outlined in the legislative provisions.

What is clear, is that the definition of consent must continue to evolve to meet the changing needs and standards of the international community.

Index

For Product Safety Concerns and Information please contact our EU representative GPSR@taylorandfrancis.com
Taylor & Francis Verlag GmbH, Kaufingerstraße 24, 80331 München, Germany

www.ingramcontent.com/pod-product-compliance
Ingram Content Group UK Ltd.
Pitfield, Milton Keynes, MK11 3LW, UK
UKHW021245190926
475569UK00001BA/5
* 9 7 8 0 3 6 7 7 1 0 7 0 5 *